REGENTS RESTORATION DRAMA SERIES

General Editor: John Loftis

SHE WOULD IF SHE COULD

D1232339

SIR GEORGE ETHEREGE

She Would If She Could

Edited by

CHARLENE M. TAYLOR

EDWARD ARNOLD

Regents Restoration Drama Series

The Regents Restoration Drama Series provides soundly edited texts, in modern spelling, of the more significant plays of the late seventeenth and early eighteenth centuries. The word "Restoration" is here used ambiguously and must be explained. A strict definition of the word is unacceptable to everyone, for it would exclude, among many other plays, those of Congreve. If to the historian it refers to the period between 1660 and 1685 (or 1688), it has long been used by the student of drama in default of a more precise term to refer to plays belonging to the dramatic tradition established in the 1660s, weakening after 1700, and displaced in the 1730s. It is in this extended sense—imprecise though justified by academic custom—that the word is used in this series, which includes plays first produced between 1660 and 1737. Although these limiting dates are determined by political events, the return of Charles II (and the removal of prohibitions against operation of theaters) and the passage of Walpole's Stage Licensing Act, they enclose a period of dramatic history having a coherence of its own in the establishment, development, and disintegration of a tradition.

The editors have planned the series with attention to the projected dimensions of the completed whole, a representative collection of Restoration drama providing a record of artistic achievement and providing also a record of the deepest concerns of three generations of Englishmen. And thus it contains deservedly famous plays—*The Country Wife*, *The Man of Mode*, and *The Way of the World*—and also significant but little known plays, *The Virtuoso*, for example, and *City Politiques*, the former a satirical review of scientific investigation in the early years of the Royal Society, the latter an equally satirical review of politics at the time of the Popish Plot. If the volumes of famous plays finally achieve the larger circulation, the other volumes may have the greater utility, in making available texts otherwise difficult of access with the editorial apparatus needed to make them intelligible.

The editors have had the instructive example of the parallel and senior project, the Regents Renaissance Drama Series; they have in fact used the editorial policies developed for the earlier plays as their own, modifying them as appropriate for the later period and as the experience of successive editions suggested. The introductions to the separate Restoration plays differ considerably in their nature. Although a uniform body of relevant information is presented in each of them, no attempt has been made to impose a pattern of interpretation. Emphasis in the introductions has necessarily varied with the nature of the plays and inevitably—we think desirably—with the special interests and aptitudes of the different editors.

Each text in the series is based on a fresh collation of the seventeenth- and eighteenth-century editions that might be presumed to have authority. The textual notes, which appear above the rule at the bottom of each page, record all substantive departures from the edition used as the copy-text. Variant substantive readings among contemporary editions are listed there as well. Editions later than the eighteenth century are referred to in the textual notes only when an emendation originating in some one of them is received into the text. Variants of accidentals (spelling, punctuation, capitalization) are not recorded in the notes except in instances in which they have, or may have, substantive relevance. Contracted forms of characters' names are silently expanded in speech prefixes and stage directions and, in the case of speech prefixes, are regularized. Additions to the stage directions of the copy-text are enclosed in brackets.

Spelling has been modernized along consciously conservative lines, but within the limits of a modernized text the linguistic quality of the original has been carefully preserved. Contracted preterites have regularly been expanded. Punctuation has been brought into accord with modern practices. The objective has been to achieve a balance between the pointing of the old editions and a system of punctuation which, without overloading the text with exclamation marks, semicolons, and dashes, will make the often loosely flowing verse and prose of the original syntactically intelligible to the modern reader. Dashes are regularly used only to indicate interrupted speeches, or shifts of address within a single speech.

Explanatory notes, chiefly concerned with glossing obsolete words and phrases, are printed below the textual notes at the bottom of each page. References to stage directions in the notes follow the admirable system of the Revels editions, whereby stage directions are keyed, decimally, to the line of the text before or after which they occur. Thus, a note on 0.2 has reference to the second line of the stage direction at the beginning of the scene in question. A note on 115.1 has reference to the first line of the stage direction following line 115 of the text of the relevant scene. Speech prefixes, and any stage directions attached to them, are keyed to the first line of accompanying dialogue.

JOHN LOFTIS

Stanford University

Contents

List of Abbreviations

Brett-Smith	H. F. B. Brett-Smith, ed. *The Dramatic Works of Sir George Etherege*. 2 vols. Oxford, 1927.
OED	*Oxford English Dictionary*
om.	omitted
Q1 corr.	Quarto, 1668; copies in Harvard, Yale, and Huntington libraries
Q1 uncorr.	Quarto, 1668; copy in Bodleian Library, Oxford
Q2	Quarto, 1671
Q3	Quarto, 1693
Verity	A. Wilson Verity, ed. *The Works of Sir George Etherege*. London, 1888.

Introduction

Sir George Etherege's second play, *She Would If She Could*, exhibits few textual problems. The first quarto (1668) is probably closest of the available texts to his manuscript and has been used as the copy-text for this edition; but that Etherege supervised even the printing of this edition is questionable, since the play was entered in the Stationers' Register on June 24, 1668, and he left London in August of that year to serve as Secretary to the Ambassador in Constantinople.[1] A second, carelessly printed quarto appeared in 1671; both the state of the text and the fact that Etherege did not return from Turkey until late in that year[2] suggest that he was not responsible for any of the variations. A third quarto appeared in 1693, two years after his death; the appearance of this quarto as well as of editions of his two other plays in the same year might indicate that they should be regarded as memorial editions. There were a number of subsequent editions during the eighteenth century, but since they could have no authorial significance, they have not been included in the collation for this edition. Four copies of the first quarto (Q1) and three copies of the second quarto (Q2) have been collated. On the unlikely chance that Etherege left some notes of revision with the printer before he departed for Ratisbon in 1685, one copy of the third quarto (Q3) has been collated. Reference has been made for the few variant passages to the editions of Verity (1888) and of Brett-Smith (1927).

The theatrical history of *She Would If She Could* is curious. The first performance at the Duke's Theater on February 6, 1667/8, was hardly successful. Although Pepys reports that one thousand people were turned away from the opening, he goes

[1] H. F. B. Brett-Smith, Introduction to *The Dramatic Works of Sir George Etherege*, I (Oxford, 1927), p. xviii.
[2] Ibid., p. xx.

on to describe the play as "a silly dull thing, though there was something very roguish and witty; but the design of the play, and the end, mighty insipid." He remarks that Etherege, who was in the pit, was displeased with the actors, who "had not their parts perfect."[3] How much weight we should allow to Pepys' critical pronouncements is debatable; he was certainly swayed in other instances by what the audience, particularly members of the Court, thought about a play.[4] Several dramatists speak favorably of *She Would If She Could*, and attribute its cool reception to the presentation rather than to any weakness in the play itself. Shadwell, three years later in the Preface to *The Humourists*, calls *She Would If She Could* "the best comedy that has been written since the Restauration of the Stage";[5] and John Dennis, in 1702, mentions the initial adverse reaction to Etherege's play while excusing the relative failure of his own adaptation of *The Merry Wives of Windsor*.[6] The play ought to have succeeded; it certainly had a brilliant opening cast. Sir Oliver was played by Harris, Sir Joslin by Nokes, Lady Cockwood by Mrs. Shadwell, Courtall by Smith, Freeman by Young, Ariana by Mrs. Jennings, and Gatty by Mrs. Davies. But only twelve performances of the play are recorded in *The London Stage* for the years between 1668 and 1680.[7] Although it is likely that other, unrecorded performances were given, *She Would If She Could* never had a towering success during Etherege's lifetime. The play fared much better during the eighteenth century, at least to judge by surviving records; there were fifty-five performances between 1705 and 1736, many of them benefits for an individual actor, a circumstance which suggests that actors thought well of the drawing

---

[3] *The Diary of Samuel Pepys*, ed. H. B. Wheatley, VII (London, 1900), p. 308.

[4] See Helen McAfee, *Pepys on the Restoration Stage* (New Haven, 1916), pp. 25–26, for a discussion of Pepys' changing attitudes.

[5] Thomas Shadwell, Preface to *The Humourists* in *The Complete Works of Thomas Shadwell*, ed. Montague Summers, I (London, 1927), p. 183.

[6] John Dennis, Epistle Dedicatory to *The Comical Gallant: or the Amours of Sir John Falstaff*, cited in Brett-Smith, *Works*, I, p. xviii.

[7] Emmett L. Avery, et al., *The London Stage, 1660–1800*, 5 pts. in 11 vols., (Carbondale, Ill., 1960–1968).

power of the play. After this time, it slipped from notice, and only two more performances, one in 1750 and one in 1751, are noted in *The London Stage*. But the theatrical history of the play should not be accepted, in this case, as the measure of its importance.

A careful reading of the play suggests that whatever weaknesses it has in construction, its significance in a consideration of the comedy of this period is great. If we are to appreciate the importance of Etherege's second comedy, we must see it in relation to its own particular type of comedy—the distinctive comedy of the Restoration:[8] more precisely, the best comedies written by men like Etherege himself, Wycherley, Congreve, Vanbrugh, and Farquhar. And in order to see it in this perspective, we must attempt to account for the particular quality, or blend of qualities, which sets Restoration comedy apart.

It is first, and most obviously, social comedy. If, as has often been claimed,[9] the comedy reflects the brilliant if sometimes debauched society of the time of Charles II, it is more concerned with contemporary social issues and problems than was formerly recognized. The comedy is set, almost exclusively, in contemporary London—and a London which is brought far more vividly before our eyes than the occasional views of a quasi-London in earlier comedy. More important, the comedy has specific relevance to the world of its day, though it is more than merely topical in its themes. Restoration dramatists, much more than those who followed them, wrote satiric comedy focused on problems in their society. We find satiric characterizations of foppish social climbers and pretenders or of ex-Commonwealth men turned ardent cavaliers. Even characters who serve other functions, such as Mel-

---

[8] This comedy has been characterized or described in a number of ways—comedy of manners, comedy of wit, the first modern comedy, to mention some of the phrases. But all of these titles, while useful in some ways, also have limitations, notably of seeming to exclude qualities present in the plays. Consequently, in this discussion, I have chosen to use simply a chronological term—Restoration comedy.

[9] See especially John Palmer, *The Comedy of Manners* (London, 1913); Bonamy Dobrée, *Restoration Comedy 1660–1720* (Oxford, 1924); and Henry Ten Eyck Perry, *The Comic Spirit in Restoration Drama* (New Haven, 1925).

antha in Dryden's *Marriage à La Mode,* are frequently fashioned to comment on those who try to intrude where they do not belong. Few Restoration comedies are without one or more interlopers. The social climber is, of course, a comic stereotype, but examination of such characters in Restoration comedy sets them somewhat apart from the type. The satire directed at them is more biting than is usual, and it is satire clearly directed at a contemporary problem.[10] Turning to histories of the period, one can understand the uneasiness of the dramatists. This was a society with an emigré mentality, fearful of being thrust once more from the sun; the Court, as well as a great many other royalists, mistakenly expected Charles's restoration to bring a return to the older status quo. As society's ranks began to stabilize, satire of social climbers tended to lose some of its sting, but initially, and to some extent throughout the whole period, the satire attacked a real problem.

Restoration society seems also to have been unusually interested in the changing attitudes toward sexual relationships and marriage resulting from conflict between the increasingly popular libertine philosophy and the older Christian-humanist tradition. In this age marriage, at least among many of the affluent, continued to be arranged primarily to increase the estate, though the young people usually had at least a veto right.[11] But the publication of numerous conduct books (many of which included sections on choosing a wife) suggests that even young people from affluent families were beginning to play a significant role

[10] As evidence that this figure represented a real concern of the era and was not simply a comic stereotype, consider the satire of social climbers appearing in pamphlets and conduct books such as *Remarques on the humours and conversations of the town* (London, 1673) and *Remarks upon remarques: or a vindication of the conversations of the town* (London, 1673). Rochester in "A Letter from Artemisa in Town to Cloe, in the Country," "Timon," and "Tunbridge-Wells," Oldham in "An Imitation of Horace," and Dryden in "Absalom and Achitophel" satirized those who sought to intrude.

[11] Arthur Bryant, *Restoration England* (London, 1960), pp. 54–55. See also P. F. Vernon, who has explored the marriage of convenience but not the decay of the custom in his "Marriage of Convenience and the Moral Code of Restoration Comedy," *Essays in Criticism,* XII (1962), pp. 370–387.

in the selection.[12] The Civil War, which disturbed social customs, may have also encouraged the young to act for themselves. In any case, clandestine marriage, during the Restoration period, became such a serious problem that attempts were made in Parliament to punish those who married sons or daughters of their masters and to raise the legal age of marriage.[13] While love and marriage are the traditional subject matter of comedy, their treatment by Restoration dramatists again suggests a vital social concern rather than a strictly conventional treatment of stock situations. The dramatists attack the marriage of convenience, but also explore more fully, and from different assumptions than in earlier periods, the nature of the total relationship between the sexes.

A combination of idealism and skepticism produced in the Restoration dramatists, and in the audiences who attended their plays, a curious double vision. Restoration audiences were quite capable of applauding the constancy of an Almanzor or an Aureng-Zebe on one day, and the next of laughing at a Loveit for expecting constancy from a Dorimant, or of reveling in a Horner's ability to manipulate the fools around him. The best dramatists of this period see very clearly the dual nature of man— half angel, half animal—and their insight raises ironic laughter. Restoration comedies are, in one sense, sparkling reflections of the society which helped to produce them—but the mirror of Restoration comic dramatists has something of the fun house in it. It enlarges and distorts the nuances of life in order to make an ironic or satiric comment about the nature of man and his society.

If the plays are social comedy, they are also romantic comedy, although not quite like that of earlier periods. It is the Restoration which develops, as John Harrington Smith calls them, "the

[12] For a discussion of conduct books on marriage see John Halkett, *Milton and the Idea of Matrimony* (New Haven, 1970), especially Chapter 2, "Fitness: the Conception of the Ideal Mate." D. R. M. Wilkinson in *The Comedy of Habit* (Leiden, 1964) also indicates, especially in Appendix A, the number of conduct books being published; unfortunately his interpretations of the plays are weak.

[13] David Ogg, *England in the Reigns of James II and William III* (Oxford, 1955), p. 76.

gay couple."[14] Most Restoration comedies make use of the basic comic plot; as the cliché has it, boy meets girl, boy loses girl, boy gets girl. But Restoration heroes and heroines differ from those who precede or follow them. They move in a constricted, convention-bound world; but they are not so unconscious of the constrictions as critics such as Kathleen Lynch suggest.[15] In many of the comedies there is a curious fusion of the heroic ideals of romance, found in the serious drama, with the realities of London life. Sometimes, as in Etherege's first play, the fusion does not take place; there, separate visions are distinguished by different forms of language and by different plot lines. As Etherege and the other dramatists grew more skillful, however, this simple juxtaposition of worlds gave way to the characteristic dual vision of man. The plays are, consequently, able to take up more serious questions and to make more complex statements than are usually found in traditional romantic comedy. Although Dryden, for example, explores the question of fashionable marriage in *Marriage à la Mode* using juxtaposition, his analysis is neither so perceptive nor so complex as the considerations of the same subject by Congreve or Farquhar, whose comic visions are not fragmented.

The development of the witty hero and heroine is, in part, a consequence of the social nature of the comedy. Such comedy demands intelligent and perceptive characters who can wear the mask of society gracefully, but who never forget that the mask and the face are not quite the same. Restoration wits, though they are not necessarily moral exempla, serve as touchstones for testing the values and assumptions of other characters; but their proximity to the dupes, which allows them to function as exposers, also brings the assumptions and actions of the wits under satiric scrutiny. Restoration dramatists are much too conscious of the real world to have an unambiguously comic vision; they and their characters are too much aware of the

[14] *The Gay Couple in Restoration Comedy* (Cambridge, Massachusetts, 1948).

[15] Kathleen M. Lynch, *The Social Mode of Restoration Comedy* (New York, 1926). See especially Chapters VI, "The Period of Etherege," and VII, "Congreve."

realities of life in a social world—of the necessity for an estate and of the dual nature of man—to believe fully either in heroic ideals or in what Frye calls the "green world" of comedy.[16] Whether they amuse themselves with the Platonic mode, with heroic ideals, or with fashionable skepticism, they never forget the realities which underlie conventional behavior. The dramatists, and the characters they create, are aware that in the real world the young hero does not always get the girl and the money.

Because the dramatists are so conscious of the dual nature of man, their plays are distinguished frequently by an unusual type of ending—the tentative or ironic resolution. A good deal of critical speculation has been raised by the endings of some of the plays; what are the prospects of a union between Harriet and Dorimant, for example, and how are we to regard the final speech of Manly in *The Plain Dealer*? It is the undercutting of romanticism which demands the distinctive characters and the unresolved conclusion. To tack the traditional comic ending onto a play of this type would be to falsify the vision of the dramatist.

It is curious that plays which have been defended against charges of immorality on the grounds that they are simply an accurate recording of the life of the times have also been defended against the same charges on the grounds that they do not appeal to moral judgment because they are obviously artificial—a "cloud cuckoo land."[17] The fact that the plays warrant, to some extent, both lines of defense suggests that they are not so simple as they have sometimes been thought to be and leads us to a consideration of a third quality of Restoration comedy. Recently, several critics[18] have commented on the dramatists' careful insistence, through the use of devices which call attention to the "playness" of the creation, that we regard the play as artifact. The most

---

[16] Northrop Frye, *Anatomy of Criticism* (Princeton, 1957), pp. 182–183.

[17] Charles Lamb, "On the Artificial Comedy of the Last Century," in *The Works of Charles and Mary Lamb*, ed. E. V. Lucas, II (London, 1903), pp. 166–167.

[18] The insistence of most critics since and including Fujimura that we examine the plays carefully suggests this point; for a more specific, if brief, discussion see Gerald Weales, Introduction to *The Complete Plays of William Wycherley* (New York, 1967), pp. xvii–xviii.

obvious example of such a device is probably the critique of *The Country Wife* included in *The Plain Dealer*. Minor but very frequent examples can be noticed—among others, references to the theater, to the conventions of drama, and to the activities of the audience. Furthermore, the playwrights, in meeting the popular demand for songs and dances, called attention to the artificiality of their creation. Though the songs, at least in the best works, have some thematic relevance, the dramatists make only the slightest attempts to introduce them realistically. Hippolita in Wycherley's *The Gentleman Dancing-Master* introduces one song with the comment, "She's come, as if she came expressly to sing the new Song she sung last night, I must hear it, for 'tis to my purpose now."[19] If one admits, as almost all critics do, the skill of Restoration dramatists in constructing dialogue, such apparent awkwardness begins to look like a deliberate accentuation of a convention. Asides and soliloquies, although long-established theatrical conventions, are sometimes turned to this use. Restoration comic dramatists characteristically blend realism and artificiality—two apparently mutually exclusive qualities. They encourage the audience, by the deliberate use of intrusive devices, to recognize that what they see on the stage is not precisely reality and thus they force the audience to go beyond simple emotional participation to thought and judgment. The strategy is, in a way, a kind of early version of Brecht's *Verfremdung* effect and is used for precisely the same purpose.

If I had to pick the single most distinctive quality of Restoration comedy, I would describe it as intellectual comedy.[20] Restoration dramatists create a complex world for the spectator or reader to evaluate, but they preach no obvious morality. They

[19] William Wycherley, *The Gentleman Dancing-Master* in *The Complete Plays of William Wycherley*, ed. Weales, p. 168.

[20] Not that all Jacobean or Caroline comedy is slapstick or even elevated farce; but *The Silent Woman*, to which Dryden pays tribute, is a relatively simple affair when compared with the best of the Restoration comedies. And certainly sentimental comedy is anti-intellectual; the least touch of the inquiring mind destroys the fragile fabric of the dramatic world in those plays, and makes one see Bevil in *The Conscious Lovers*, for example, as a self-blinded, self-righteous prig rather than as the exemplary hero Steele intended.

seldom, for example, have an authorial spokesman; Wycherley is neither Horner nor Manly, and what Wycherley says is said in the whole of the play rather than by any single character. Several recent critics[21] indicate the importance of seeing these plays as intellectual comedy, as the outgrowth of both Renaissance humanism and the skeptical temperament of the age. Restoration dramatists create plays which, through the fusion of the social, romantic, and artificial elements, demand that the audience think about and evaluate the action and the characters. Thus, whether they use satire to expose the follies or vices of their age in the persons of fops and social pretenders, or whether they call for an ironic awareness of the nature of man through the relationship established between hero and dupe, the dramatists exercise the intelligence of the reader or spectator.

The primary demand for intellectual awareness rather than emotional participation is a corollary of the remarkable language of Restoration comedy. The dramatists are, in some respects, the inheritors of the metaphysical poets. The simile, a favorite rhetorical device of the period, is frequently used in an almost metaphysical way to insist on generally unperceived relationships. The language of the plays becomes an instrument of evaluation. The would-be wits, for example, pride themselves on making similes; but since their similes are only obvious comparisons, they reveal the poverty of their intelligence.

The demands for intelligent and perceptive audiences are, of course, hazardous. As Restoration comedy developed, and as society changed, the presence of guides becomes more obvious. Early Restoration dramatists rely, almost exclusively, on the perception of the audience; but by the time Congreve and Farquhar were writing, indications of moral norms are far more clear. Mirabel and Millamant more closely approximate the roles of authorial spokesmen and moral norms than do Harriet and Dorimant. Although later Restoration comedies presented a com-

[21] See especially Thomas Fujimura, *The Restoration Comedy of Wit* (Princeton, 1952); Dale Underwood, *Etherege and the Seventeenth Century Comedy of Manners* (New Haven and Oxford, 1957); and Jocelyn Powell "George Etherege and the Form of a Comedy," in *Stratford-upon-Avon Studies*, VI (1965), pp. 43–69.

plex world and called for judgment, they did not, unfortunately, always get it. Congreve was, for example, accused of making his fools speak like wits.

Restoration comedy gains its distinctive nature, then, from its fusion of social, romantic, artificial, and intellectual strains. Several plays have been suggested as "the first example of Restoration comedy," but most of them were merely comedies written early in the Restoration period; that is, they do not achieve the blend of the four qualities, although some of the elements of Restoration comedy may be present. The comedies which have been most frequently suggested are Cowley's *The Cutter of Coleman-Street* (1661); Sir Robert Howard's *The Committee* (1662); James Howard's *The English Monsieur* (1663); Etherege's own first play, *The Comical Revenge* (1664); and Dryden's *Secret Love* (1667).

In none of these five does the characteristic fusion occur, although all of them have some elements typical of Restoration comedy. Cowley's play has no characters who correspond to the witty lovers, many of the characterizations are more typically Jonsonian than Restoration, and its setting, interests, and assumptions are those of the Interregnum rather than of the Restoration. Sir Robert Howard, although he uses perceptive heroines, does not use them in the typical pattern of Restoration lovers, and his play is more concerned with exposing the hypocrisy of Puritans than with the problems which are those of the Restoration dramatists. James Howard's *The English Monsieur* and Etherege's *The Comical Revenge* have disqualifications in common. In both plays, the heroines are widows, and given the age's attitude toward widows, the courtships are more boisterous and less witty than those characteristic of Restoration comedy. Dryden's *Secret Love* and Etherege's first play are both in part in the heroic style, including passages written in verse and having, to some extent, the code of the heroic world rather than the fusion of heroic ideals with comic reality characteristic of Restoration comedy. Though all of these plays have been suggested by various critics, Etherege's second play, *She Would If She Could,* has been more often, without much explanation,[22] referred to as the first example of the new comedy. If we examine it in the light of the criteria already set forth, we shall have the basis for a better evaluation. The dramatic world which Etherege creates in this play is the contemporary world of London, or at least of the most significant part, politically and socially; scenes are set, for example, in the New Exchange, in the New Spring Gardens, and in popular taverns. The *beau monde* of Etherege's London serves as a model for the milieu Etherege creates for his characters; visits to the Exchange, to the plays, to the taverns were all a part of London of the 1660s. But Etherege's purpose in creating this world so vividly is more complex than simply the novelty of holding a mirror up to his society; the assumptions on which the play is based are related to some of the social concerns of the period, particularly to the uneasiness about social intruders. The dupes in this play have been constructed as more than simple blocking figures. Thus, Sir Oliver's statement about his coming to town, that he was "e'en grown a sot for want of gentleman-like recreations" (I.i.79), is used by Etherege as part of the indication of Sir Oliver's social pretension. Although he amply demonstrates himself to be what the heroes call him, "an oaf" (I.i.250), he is an oaf who pretends to the libertine philosophy of the town and whose exposure in the tavern scene (III.iii) reveals his physical, mental, and social incapacity to play such a role. In addition, his name (since he would normally be called by title plus Christian name) is an indicative one; Oliver, of course, suggests Puritanism, and by extension Puritan hypocrisy. But Etherege is no longer interested so much in whatever Puritan element his dupes may have (as indicated by his fuller exploration of this point in the characterization of Sir Nicholas Cully in *The Comical Revenge*) but only in Sir Oliver's intrusion into a society where he does not belong. Thus, he makes Sir Oliver less of a fool, and therefore more of a threat than the earlier character. The characterization of Sir Oliver's crony helps to support this thesis. If Sir Joslin's actions are, in some respects, very much like those of his friend, he is,

[22] H. F. B. Brett-Smith, for example, in his Introduction to Etherege's *Works*, calls him the founder of a new type of comedy (I, lxix) but does not specify *She Would If She Could* as the first example of it.

finally, less the butt of satiric laughter because, unlike Sir Oliver, he does not pretend to be what he is not. He is a bluff, hearty, if foolish country gentleman, but a well-meaning and good-hearted one; his treatment in this play prefigures the treatment of Sir Wilful in Congreve's *The Way of the World*.

Lady C.

By far the strongest satire of the play is turned against Lady Cockwood. She is the forerunner of a number of longing ladies like Loveit, Fidget, and Wishfort; but her characterization is not simply that of an older, married woman chasing all younger, single men. Her hypocrisy is so habitual that she can no longer be honest either with her confederates (II.ii.95–99) or with herself (I.ii.1–4). Significantly, her physical desires are interwined with her conception of heroic love and honor, giving us ample indication of her role as social pretender. She refers, for example, to Courtall as "heroic sir" (III.i.182), and it is her insistence on following the heroic code of behavior which allows Courtall to continue to frustrate her physical desires. Though she escapes a complete exposure scene within the world of the play (at least partially because it suits the heroes' plans to protect her), she has been effectively exposed to the audience. Her statement of retirement, "It has made me so truly sensible of those dangers to which an aspiring lady must daily expose her honor, that I am resolved to give over the great business of this town, and hereafter modestly confine myself to the humble affairs of my own family," (V.567–571) and her following complaint, "Certainly fortune was never before so unkind to the ambition of a lady," (V.574–575) are used by Etherege as the final confirmation of her more complex role. She aspires to play the role of a witty heroine, a role for which she is qualified neither by marital status, age, nor perception.

These characters illustrate the strengths and weaknesses of the society Etherege saw around him. It is a world of wits and fools. If the questions he opens in this play are not so complex as those of later Restoration drama, the picture of man in society which Etherege exhibits here is sufficiently perceptive to anticipate the development of the more sophisticated considerations of the later plays.

She Would If She Could also has, for the first time, the characteristic blend of the romantic element. Courtall and Freeman are true Restoration gallants—witty, perceptive, libertine, though not without honor. And they are not limited in perception as is Sir Frederick in Etherege's earlier play; there is no danger that these gallants will consider noise and window-breaking to be an indication of wit. Their allegiance to libertine principles is indicated by Freeman's early statement that they had best plan to "follow the old trade: eat well, and prepare ourselves with a bottle or two of good Burgundy that our old acquaintance may look lovely in our eyes . . ." (I.i.4–7). But their libertine' principles are not simply a rationalization of lust; Courtall, we soon learn, is in real, if decorous, flight from Lady Cockwood. All cats are not, for these heroes, the same in the dark. Like typical Restoration heroes, they are as interested in the chase as in the capture. Their typically libertine attempt to carry on two intrigues simultaneously nearly lands them in difficulty (since the girls in both intrigues are quickly revealed to be the same), but their adherence to libertinism is strongly qualified by their pragmatic attitude toward the sexual relationship and marriage, implied by their announced position at the end of the play, "A pretty country seat, madam, with a handsome parcel of land, and other necessaries belonging to't, may tempt us; but for a town tenement that has but one poor conveniency, we are resolved we'll never deal" (V.462–465).

Etherege's most significant innovation in this aspect of Restoration comedy is the use of the characteristic witty heroine, or, in this case, heroines. Gatty and Ariana, unlike the widow of the earlier play, are single, emancipated women—well aware of their own value and able to meet the gallants on equal terms. They are also very much ladies of this time and place and consequently not scented with the faint air of unreality which hangs over Florimel in Dryden's *Secret Love*. In their opening scene they declare for liberty, but also for being "mighty honest" (I.ii.153). What distinguishes them most significantly from the dupe, Lady Cockwood, is that they are basically honest with themselves; Gatty says: "I hate to dissemble when I need not. 'Twould look as affected in us to be reserved now we're alone as for a player to maintain the character she acts in the tiring room" (V.304–307). They can recognize the difference between dissimulation, which is necessary in society and which involves a consciousness of the mask, and affectation or hypocrisy, in which the character loses the ability to distinguish between mask and face. These two girls, though not as carefully drawn as some of the later, great heroines, are clearly Restoration heroines. They are generally at least as successful, for example, in the courtship game as are the gallants; they contrive a further meeting without acceding to the gallants' demands for revelation of their identities (II.i), they discomfort Courtall (even more than they know) in the Exchange scene (III.i), they certainly hold their own in refuting the charges of the gallants in the park scene (IV.ii), and they are able to turn their encounters to a final advantage in insisting on their own terms—marriage.

In the final scene we also find the characteristic tentative or ironic resolution, unlike the purely comic resolution of Etherege's earlier play. These girls put the gallants under a month's probation, and although it seems likely they will marry, Freeman's comment, "A month is a tedious time, and will be a dangerous trial of our resolutions; but I hope we shall not repent before marriage, whate'er we do after" (V.515–517), strikes an ironic note. The irony is deepened even more when Etherege then turns to the Cockwood marriage and gives to Sir Oliver the final lines of the play, which celebrate the reunion of the Cockwoods. The relationship between the sexes, then, is a complex one, calling for perception and judgment, and Etherege refuses to falsify his vision of human nature.

Although Etherege enjoyed affecting the role of the cultured gentleman who tossed off plays for his recreation and cultivated a reputation for laziness, a careful reading of his plays suggests that they are more carefully constructed than might be supposed. In *She Would If She Could,* he uses several techniques to insist that the audience recognize that his play is not simply a faithful re-creation of life, but rather a work of art. His use of songs, for example, is far more sophisticated than in his first play. In *The Comical Revenge,* most of the songs occur in one scene and are part of the mask of the simple country dweller which Palmer

assumes in order to gull Sir Nicholas; in *She Would If She Could,*
the twelve songs are scattered throughout the play. Most of them,
it is true, function as characterization of Sir Joslin; but they
frequently have thematic relevance and are carefully woven into
the fabric of the play. Sir Joslin's song after the discovery in the
tavern,

> Love and wenching are toys,
> Fit to please beardless boys,
> They're sports we hate worse than a Leaguer;
> When we visit a miss,
> We still brag how we kiss,
> But 'tis with a bottle we feague her.
>
> (III.iii.381–386)

is used, for example, to help lull Lady Cockwood's ruffled sus-
picions, but also, ironically, to provide an accurate comment
on Sir Oliver's sexual incapacity to play the libertine role. Gatty's
song in the last act functions almost like a soliloquy, as an indication of her true feelings. But, though these songs have thematic
relevance, one must note that Etherege makes only the scantiest
attempt to introduce them smoothly. Gatty, for example, introduces hers with the comment, "How I love the song I learnt
t'other day, since I saw them in the Mulberry Garden" (V.289–
290). Here, then, is the typical Restoration insistence on the
artificiality of the work in order to call for judgment from the
audience.

Etherege also uses stage conventions, particularly the aside, to
insist on the artifice of his creation. His skill in using them is
greater than in his earlier play, and much more in line with
typical Restoration practice. For example, Mrs. Sentry comments
in an aside on her mistress's behavior, "If I stay in the room, she
will not speak kindly to me in a week after; and if I go out, she
always chides me thus. This is a strange infirmity she has, but I
must bear with it; for on my conscience, custom has made it so
natural, she cannot help it" (II.ii.95–99). This information is
neither new nor necessary to the plot, but is used rather to point
out that Lady Cockwood's appearance and her reality are different
and to call for judgment on those who can no longer distinguish

between the face and the mask. Etherege has no single authorial spokesman in the play: he can use stage conventions to make his comment.

Still another technique is the use of frequent, if scattered, references to the performance of plays, to players, and even to his own first work. Gatty's previously quoted speech on the appropriateness of dissimulation includes the phrase, "as for a player to maintain the character she acts in the tiring room" (V.305–307). Etherege, thus, suddenly makes us aware that what we are seeing is, in fact, a player playing a role. Even the more minor references, such as those to the gentleman's diversion of seeing plays, especially without paying for them (IV.i.10–11), while dramatically appropriate, serve to remind the audience that they are watching a play, not reality. Although Rake-hell's speech, "'Slife, love in a cap is more ridiculous than love in a tub, or love in a pipkin" (III.iii.108–110), is appropriate in its context, the reference to the sub-title of Etherege's first play jerks us suddenly out of the world of this play and back into the world of reality. Throughout his play Etherege uses devices which insist on the artifice of the creation in order to call attention to the need for perception and judgment on the part of the audience—devices that are part of the Restoration style and that help to give Restoration comedy its distinctive flavor.

She Would If She Could does not make the complex demands of some of the later Restoration plays, but it clearly makes intellectual demands on its audience. The characteristic three elements of social, romantic, and artificial comedy create and insist upon the intellectual quality of this comedy. The world which Etherege creates is complex. If one can pick out typical elements, such as the satire of aspiring fools as they function as foils to the skill and perception of the wits, the play as a whole is yet greater than the sum of its parts. Courtall, for example, is perceptive and witty enough to be able to manipulate Lady Cockwood, since he knows she cannot distinguish between mask and face; but he is bound, to some extent, by his own acceptance of the social world. His discomfiture in dealing with the girls in Act IV is traceable directly to the game in which he is not an entirely willing player. The reaction Etherege calls for, throughout the play, is the intelligent recognition of life's complexity. Evaluation and judgment of the merits of the assumptions made and actions taken by the characters is perhaps implicit in the play. If, as with most Restoration comedies, it is possible to see this play as simply an amusing, entertaining work of sophisticated humor, there are also indications of complexity which warn the careful reader or thoughtful spectator that Etherege has more to say than the surface of his play reveals. It is all this which makes *She Would If She Could* typical of Restoration comedy, and important because here for the first time the peculiar, fascinating, and even challenging world of Restoration comedy has been fully created.

It is a pleasure to thank the English Department of the University of Arizona for the funds and for the secretarial help which made this edition possible.

CHARLENE M. TAYLOR

University of Arizona

SHE WOULD IF SHE COULD

DRAMATIS PERSONAE

SIR OLIVER COCKWOOD
SIR JOSLIN JOLLEY } *two country knights*

MR. COURTALL
MR. FREEMAN } *two honest gentlemen of the town*   5

MY LADY COCKWOOD

ARIANA
GATTY } *two young ladies, kinswomen of Sir Joslin Jolley*   10

MRS. SENTRY, *my Lady Cockwood's gentlewoman*

MRS. GAZETTE
MRS. TRINKET } *two Exchange-Women*

MR. RAKE-HELL, *a knight of the industry*   15

THOMAS, *Sir Oliver Cockwood's man*

A SERVANT *belonging to Mr. Courtall*

WAITERS, FIDDLERS, AND OTHER ATTENDANTS

---

13. *Exchange-Women*] women who had shops in the New Exchange, a two-story arcade, built 1608–1609, housing the shops of drapers, mercers, seamstresses, and milliners; a fashionable shopping and gossiping area.

15. *knight of the industry*] a sharper or swindler; here also a pimp.

She Would If She Could

A dining room. Enter Courtall *and* Freeman, *and a* Servant *brushing* Courtall.

COURTALL.

So, so, 'tis well. Let the coach be made ready.

SERVANT.

It shall, sir.

Exit Servant.

COURTALL.

Well, Frank, what is to be done today?

FREEMAN.

Faith, I think we must e'en follow the old trade: eat
well, and prepare ourselves with a bottle or two of good   5
Burgundy that our old acquaintance may look lovely
in our eyes; for, for aught as I see, there is no hopes
of new.

COURTALL.

Well! This is grown a wicked town. It was otherwise in
my memory. A gentleman should not have gone out of   10
his chamber, but some civil officer or other of the game
would have been with him, and have given him notice
where he might have had a course or two in the afternoon.

FREEMAN.

Truly a good motherly woman of my acquaintance   15
t'other day, talking of the sins of the times, told me,
with tears in her eyes, that there are a company of higling

rascals, who partly for themselves, but more especially
for some secret friends, daily forestall the markets; nay,

---

13. *course*] pursuit or hunt.
17. *higling*] striving for petty advantage in bargaining.

and that many gentlemen who formerly had been persons   20
of great worth and honor, are of late, for some private
reasons, become their own purveyors, to the utter decay
and disencouragement of trade and industry.

COURTALL.

I know there are some wary merchants who never trust
their business to a factor; but for my part, I hate the   25
fatigue, and had rather be bound to back my own colts,
and man my own hawks, than endure the impertinencies
of bring a young wench to the lure.

Enter Servant.

SERVANT.

Sir, there is a gentlewoman below desires to speak with
you.   30

COURTALL.

Ha, Freeman, this may be some lucky adventure.

SERVANT.

She asked me if you were alone.

COURTALL.

And did not you say aye?

SERVANT.

I told her I would go see.

COURTALL.

Go, go down quickly, and tell her I am. Frank, prithee   35
let me put thee into this closet a while.

FREEMAN.

Why, may not I see her?

COURTALL.

On my life thou shalt have fair play, and go halves, if
it be a purchase that may with honor be divided; you
may overhear all. But for decency' sake, in, in, man.   40

FREEMAN.

Well, good fortune attend thee.

Enter Mrs. Sentry.

---

26. *fatigue*] at this period a French word; the *OED* lists the first
example of the word as English in 1693.

COURTALL.

Mrs. Sentry, this is a happiness beyond my expectation.

SENTRY.

Your humble servant, sir.

COURTALL.

I hope your lady's come to town.

SENTRY.

Sir Oliver, my lady, and the whole family. Well, we have 45
had a sad time in the country; my lady's so glad she's
come to enjoy the freedom of this place again, and I
dare say longs to have the happiness of your company.

COURTALL.

Did she send you hither?

SENTRY.

Oh no. If she should but know that I did such a con- 50
fident trick, she would think me a good one i'faith.
The zeal I have to serve you made me venture to call in
my way to the Exchange to tell you the good news, and
to let you know our lodgings are in James Street at
the Black Posts, where we lay the last summer. 55

COURTALL.

Indeed it is very obligingly done.

SENTRY.

But I must needs desire you to tell my lady that you
came to the knowledge of this by some lucky chance or
other, for I would not be discovered for a world.

COURTALL.

Let me alone, I warrant thee. 60

Enter Servant.

SERVANT.

Sir Oliver Cockwood, sir, is come to wait on you.

SENTRY.

Oh Heaven! my master! my lady and myself are both
undone, undone—

COURTALL.

'Sdeath, why did you not tell him I was busy?

SENTRY.

    For Heaven's sake, Mr. Courtall, what shall I do?   65

COURTALL.

    Leave, leave trembling, and creep into the wood-hole
here.   *She goes into the wood-hole.*

                Enter Sir Oliver.

COURTALL.

    Sir Oliver Cockwood!   *Embraces him.*

SIR OLIVER.

    Honest Ned Courtall. By my troth, I think thou tak'st
me for a pretty wench, thou hugg'st me so very close   70
and heartily.

COURTALL.

    Only my joy to see you, Sir Oliver, and to welcome you
to town.

SIR OLIVER.

    Methinks, indeed, I have been an age absent, but I
intend to redeem the time. And how, and how stand   75
affairs, prithee now? Is the wine good? Are the women
kind? Well, faith, a man had better be a vagabond in
this town, than a Justice of Peace in the country. I was
e'en grown a sot for want of gentleman-like recreations.
If a man do but rap out an oath, the people start as if a   80
gun went off; and if one chance but to couple himself
with his neighbor's daughter, without the help of the
parson of the parish, and leave a little testimony of his
kindness behind him, there is presently such an uproar
that a poor man is fain to fly his country. As for drunk-   85
enness, 'tis true, it may be used without scandal, but
the drink is so abominable that a man would forbear
it, for fear of being made out of love with the vice.

COURTALL.

    I see, Sir Oliver, you continue still your old humor, and
are resolved to break your sweet lady's heart.   90

SIR OLIVER.

    You do not think me sure so barbarously unkind to let

her know all this; no, no, these are secrets fit only to be
trusted to such honest fellows as thou art.

COURTALL.

Well may I, poor sinner, be excused, since a woman
of such rare beauty, such incomparable parts, and of   95
such an unblemished reputation is not able to reclaim
you from these wild courses, Sir Oliver.

SIR OLIVER.

To say the truth, she is a wife that no man need be
ashamed of, Ned.

COURTALL.

I vow, Sir Oliver, I must needs blame you, considering 100
how tenderly she loves you.

SIR OLIVER.

Aye, aye, the more is her misfortune, and mine too,
Ned. I would willingly give thee a pair of the best coach
horses in my stable, so thou couldst but persuade her to
love me less.   105

COURTALL.

Her virtue and my friendship sufficiently secure you
against that, Sir Oliver.

SIR OLIVER.

I know thou wert never married; but has it never been
thy misfortune to have a mistress love thee thus entirely?

COURTALL.

It never has been my good fortune, Sir Oliver. But why 110
do you ask this question?

SIR OLIVER.

Because then, perchance, thou mightst have been a little
sensible what a damned trouble it is.

COURTALL.

As how, Sir Oliver?

SIR OLIVER.

Why look thee, thus: for a man cannot be altogether 115
ungrateful, sometimes one is obliged to kiss, and fawn,
and toy, and lie fooling an hour or two, when a man

114. Oliver?] *Q1, 3;* Oliver. *Q2.*

had rather, if it were not for the disgrace sake, stand
all that while in the pillory paulted with rotten eggs
and oranges.   120

COURTALL.

This is a very hard case indeed, Sir Oliver.

SIR OLIVER.

And then the inconvience of keeping regular hours.
But above all, that damned fiend jealousy does so
possess these passionate lovers, that I protest, Ned, under
the rose be it spoken, if I chance to be a little prodigal 125
in my expense on a private friend or so, I am called
to so strict an account at night, that for quietness' sake
I am often forced to take a dose of cantharides to make
up the sum.

COURTALL.

Indeed, Sir Oliver, everything considered, you are not 130
so much to be envied as one may rashly imagine.

SIR OLIVER.

Well, a pox of this tying a man and woman together,
for better, for worse! Upon my conscience it was but
a trick that the clergy might have a feeling in the cause.

COURTALL.

I do not conceive it to be much for their profit, Sir 135
Oliver, for I dare lay a good wager, let 'em but allow
Christian liberty, and they shall get ten times more by
christenings than they are likely to lose by marriages.

SIR OLIVER.

Faith, thou hast hit it right, Ned; and now thou talk'st
of Christian liberty, prithee let us dine together today, 140
and be swingingly merry, but with all secrecy.

COURTALL.

I shall be glad of your good company, Sir Oliver.

118–119. *stand . . . pillory*] a form of public punishment, related to
the stocks.

124–125. *under the rose*] i.e., *sub rosa*, confidentially.

128. *cantharides*] a preparation of powdered flies, usually used as a
diuretic but also considered an aphrodisiac.

SIR OLIVER.

I am to call on a very honest fellow, whom I left here
hard by making a visit, Sir Joslin Jolly, a kinsman of my
wife's, and my neighbor in the country; we call brothers. 145
He came up to town with me, and lodgeth in the same
house. He has brought up a couple of the prettiest kinswomen, heiresses of a very good fortune. Would thou
hadst the instructing of 'em a little; faith, if I am not
very much mistaken, they are very prone to the study 150
of mathematics.

COURTALL.

I shall be beholding to you for so good an acquaintance.

SIR OLIVER.

/ This Sir Joslin is in great favor with my lady, one that
she has an admirable good opinion of, and will trust me
with him anywhere; but to say truth, he is as arrant a 155
sinner as the best of us, and will boggle at nothing that
becomes a man of honor. We will go and get leave of my
lady; for it is not fit I should break out so soon without
her approbation, Ned.

COURTALL.

By no means, Sir Oliver. 160

SIR OLIVER.

Where shall we meet about an hour hence?

COURTALL.

At the French House or the Bear.

SIR OLIVER.

At the French House, by all means.

COURTALL.

Agreed, agreed.

SIR OLIVER.

Would thou couldst bring a fourth man. 165

COURTALL.

What think you of Frank Freeman?

---

162. *French House . . . Bear*] fashionable taverns and eating houses.

SIR OLIVER.

There cannot be a better—well—servant, Ned, servant, Ned!

COURTALL.

Your servant, Sir Oliver.

Exit Sir Oliver.

Mrs. Sentry!   170

SENTRY *(in the hole)*.

Is he gone?

COURTALL.

Aye, aye! You may venture to bolt now.

SENTRY *(crawling out)*.

Oh Heavens! I would not endure such another fright.

COURTALL.

Come, come, prithee be composed.

SENTRY.

I shall not be myself again this fortnight; I never was 175
in such a taking all the days of my life. To have been
found false, and to one who to say truth has been
always very kind and civil to me; but above all, I was
concerned for my lady's honor—

COURTALL.

Come, come. There's no harm done.   180

SENTRY.

Ah! Mr. Courtall, you do not know Sir Oliver so well
as I do. He has strange humors sometimes, and has
it enough in's nature to play the tyrant, but that my
lady and myself awe him by our policy.

COURTALL.

Well, well, all's well. Did you not hear what a tearing 185
blade Sir Oliver is?

SENTRY.

Ah! 'tis a vile dissembling man; how fairly he carries
it to my lady's face! But I dare not discover him for fear
of betraying myself.

176. all the] *Verity, Brett–Smith;*   185. tearing] *Q3;* taring *Q1–2.*
om. *Q1–3.*

---

185. *tearing*] ranting, blustering.

COURTALL.

> Well, Mrs. Sentry, I must dine with 'em, and after I 190
> have entered them with a beer glass or two, if I can I
> will slip away, and pay my respects to your lady.

SENTRY.

> You need not question your welcome, I assure you, sir.
> Your servant, sir.

COURTALL.

> Your servant, Mrs. Sentry. I am very sensible of this 195
> favor, I assure you.

SENTRY.

> I am proud it was in my power to oblige you, sir.
>
> *Exit* Sentry.

COURTALL.

> Freeman! come, come out of thy hole. How hast thou
> been able to contain?

FREEMAN.

> Faith, much ado; the scene was very pleasant. But above 200
> all, I admire thy impudence. I could never have had
> the face to have wheadled the poor knight so.

COURTALL.

> Pish, pish. 'Twas both necessary and honest; we ought
> to do all we can to confirm a husband in the good
> opinion of his wife.   205

FREEMAN.

> Pray how long, if without offense a man may ask you,
> have you been in good grace with this person of honor?
> I never knew you had that commendable quality of
> secrecy before.

COURTALL.

> You are mistaken, Freeman. Things go not as you 210
> wickedly imagine.

FREEMAN.

> Why, hast thou lost all sense of modesty? Dost thou
> think to pass these gross wheadles on me too? Come, come,
> this good news should make thee a little merrier. Faith,

---

202. *wheadled*] conned, made a fool of.

though she be an old acquaintance, she has the advan-   215
tage of four or five months' absence. 'Slid, I know not
how proud you are, but I have thought myself very
spruce ere now in an old suit that has been brushed
and laid up a while.

COURTALL.

Freeman, I know in cases of this nature thou art an   220
infidel; but yet methinks the knowledge thou hast of
my sincere dealing with my friends should make thee
a little more confiding.

FREEMAN.

What devilish oath could she invent to fright thee from
a discovery?   225

COURTALL.

Wilt thou believe me if I swear the preservation of her
honor has been my fault, and not hers?

FREEMAN.

This is something.

COURTALL.

Why then, know that I have still been as careful to
prevent all opportunities as she has been to contrive   230
'em; and still have carried it so like a gentleman, that
she has not had the least suspicion of unkindness. She
is the very spirit of impertinence, so foolishly fond and
troublesome that no man above sixteen is able to endure
her.   235

FREEMAN.

Why did you engage thus far then?

COURTALL.

Some conveniences which I had by my acquaintance
with the sot her husband made me extraordinary civil
to her, which presently by her ladyship was interpreted
after the manner of the most obliging women. This   240
wench came hither by her commission today.

FREEMAN.

With what confidence she denied it!

232. she has] *Q3, Verity;* there has *Q1-2, Brett-Smith.*

COURTALL.

Nay, that's never wanting, I assure you. Now is it
expected I should lay by all other occasions, and watch
every opportunity to wait upon her; she would by her 245
good will give her lover no more rest than a young
squire that has newly set up a coach does his only pair
of horses.

FREEMAN.

Faith, if it be as thou sayst, I cannot much blame the
hardness of thy heart. But did not the oaf talk of two 250
young ladies?

COURTALL.

Well remembered, Frank, and now I think on't, 'twill be
very necessary to carry on my business with the old one
that we may the better have an opportunity of being
acquainted with them. Come, let us go and bespeak 255
dinner, and by the way consider of these weighty
affairs.

FREEMAN.

Well, since there is but little ready money stirring,
rather than want entertainment, I shall be contented
to play a while upon tick.   260

COURTALL.

And I, provided they promise fair, and we find there's
hopes of payment hereafter.

FREEMAN.

Come along, come along.   *Exeunt.*

[I. ii]

Sir Oliver Cockwood's lodging. Enter Lady Cockwood.

LADY COCKWOOD.

'Tis too late to repent. I sent her, but yet I cannot but
be troubled to think she stays so long; sure if she has so
little gratitude to let him, he has more honor than to
attempt anything to the prejudice of my affection.

2. stays] *Q2–3;* stay's *Q1.*

---

260. *play . . . tick*] play on credit.

Enter Sentry.

Oh, Sentry, are you come?   5

SENTRY.

Oh madam! There has been such an accident!

LADY COCKWOOD.

Prithee do not frighten me, wench.

SENTRY.

As I was discoursing with Mr. Courtall, in came Sir
Oliver.

LADY COCKWOOD.

Oh! I'm ruined, undone forever!   10

SENTRY.

You'll still be sending me on these desperate errands.

LADY COCKWOOD.

I am betrayed, betrayed, by this false—what shall I call
thee?

SENTRY.

Nay, but madam, have a little patience—

LADY COCKWOOD.

I have lost all patience, and will never more have any. 15

SENTRY.

Do but hear me. All is well—

LADY COCKWOOD.

Nothing can be well, unfortunate woman.

SENTRY.

Mr. Courtall thrust me into the wood-hole.

LADY COCKWOOD.

And did not Sir Oliver see thee?

SENTRY.

He had not the least glimpse of me.   20

LADY COCKWOOD.

Dear Sentry. And what good news?

SENTRY.

He intends to wait upon you in the afternoon, madam.

LADY COCKWOOD.

I hope you did not let him know I sent you.

SENTRY.

No, no, madam. I'll warrant you I did everything much
to the advantage of your honor. 25

LADY COCKWOOD.

Ah Sentry! If we could but think of some lucky plot now
to get Sir Oliver out of the way.

SENTRY.

You need not trouble yourself about that, madam; he
has engaged to dine with Mr. Courtall at the French
House, and is bringing Sir Joslin Jolly to get your good 30
will. When Mr. Courtall has fixed 'em with a beer glass
or two, he intends to steal away, and pay his devotion to
your ladyship.

LADY COCKWOOD.

Truly, he is a person of much worth and honor.

SENTRY.

Had you but been there, madam, to have overheard 35
Sir Oliver's discourse, he would have made you bless
yourself; there is not such another wild man in the
town. All his talk was of wenching, and swearing, and
drinking, and tearing.

LADY COCKWOOD.

Aye, aye, Sentry. I know he'll talk of strange matters 40
behind my back; but if he be not an abominable hypocrite at home, and I am not a woman easily to be
deceived, he is not able to play the spark abroad thus,
I assure you.

Enter Sir Oliver *and* Sir Joslin, Sir Joslin *singing.*

My dearest dear. This is kindly done of thee to come 45
home again thus quickly.

SIR OLIVER.

Nay, my dear. Thou shalt never have any just cause to
accuse me of unkindness.

LADY COCKWOOD.

Sir Joslin, now you are a good man, and I shall trust
you with Sir Oliver again. 50

SIR JOSLIN.

 Nay, if I ever break my word with a lady, I will be
delivered bound to Mrs. Sentry here, and she shall have
leave to carve me for a capon.

SENTRY.

 Do you think I have a heart cruel enough for such a
bloody execution? 55

SIR JOSLIN.

 Kindly spoke i'faith, girl. I'll give thee a buss for
that.

LADY COCKWOOD.

 Fie, fie, Sir Joslin. This is not seemly in my presence.

SIR JOSLIN.

 We have all our failings, lady, and this is mine. A
right-bred greyhound can as well forbear running after 60
a hare when he sees her, as I can mumbling a pretty
wench when she comes in my way.

LADY COCKWOOD.

 I have heard indeed you are a parlous man, Sir Joslin.

SIR JOSLIN.

 I seldom brag, lady, but for a true cock of the game,
little Joslin dares match with the best of 'em. 65

SIR OLIVER.

 Sir Joslin's merry, my dear.

LADY COCKWOOD.

 Aye, aye. If he should be wicked, I know thou art too
much a gentleman to offer an injury to thine own dear
lady.

SIR JOSLIN.

 Faith, madam, you must give my Brother Cockwood 70
leave to dine abroad today.

LADY COCKWOOD.

 I protest, Sir Joslin, you begin to make me hate you
too. Well, you are e'en grown as bad as the worst of

---

61. *mumbling*] fondling with the lips.
63. *parlous*] dangerous, mischievous.

'em; you are still robbing me of the sweet society of
Sir Oliver.   75

SIR JOSLIN.

Come, come. Your discipline is too severe, i'faith, lady.

LADY COCKWOOD.

Sir Oliver may do what he pleases, sir. He knows I have
ever been his obedient lady.

SIR OLIVER.

Prithee, my dear, be not angry. Sir Joseph was so earnest
in his invitation that none but a clown could have   80
refused him.

SIR JOSLIN.

Aye, aye. We dine at my uncle Sir Joseph Jolly's, lady.

LADY COCKWOOD.

Will you be sure now to be a good dear, and not drink,
nor stay out late?

SIR JOSLIN.

I'll engage for all, and if there be no harm in a merry   85
catch or a waggish story—

Enter Ariana *and* Mrs. Gatty.

Ha, ha! Sly-girl and Mad-cap, are you got up? I know
what you have been meditating on; but never trouble
your heads. Let me alone to bring you consolation.

GATTY.

We have often been beholding to you, sir; for everytime   90
he's drunk, he brings us home a couple of fresh servants.

SIR OLIVER.

Well, farewell, my dear. Prithee do not sigh thus, but
make thee ready, visit, and be merry.

LADY COCKWOOD.

I shall receive most satisfaction in my chamber.

SIR JOSLIN.

Come, come along Brother. Farewell one and all, Lady   95
and Sly-girl, Sly-girl and Mad-cap, your servant, your
servant.   *Exit* Sir Oliver *and* Sir Joslin singing.

LADY COCKWOOD *(to* Sentry *aside).*

Sentry, is the new point I brought come home, and is
everything in a readiness?

SENTRY.

Everything, madam.   100

LADY COCKWOOD.

Come, come up quickly then, girl, and dress me.

Exit Lady Cockwood *and* Sentry.

ARIANA.

Dost not thou wonder, Gatty, she should be so strangely
fond of this coxcomb?

GATTY.

Well, if she does not dissemble, may I still be discovered
when I do. Didst thou not see how her countenance 105
changed, as soon as ever their backs were turned, and how
earnestly she whispered with her woman? There is some
weighty affair in hand, I warrant thee. My dear Ariana,
how glad am I we are in this town again.

ARIANA.

But we have left the benefit of the fresh air, and the 110
delight of wandering in the pleasant groves.

GATTY.

Very pretty things for a young gentlewoman to bemoan
the loss of indeed, that's newly come to a relish of the
good things of this world.

ARIANA.

Very good, sister!   115

GATTY.

Why, hast not thou promised me a thousand times to
leave off this demureness?

ARIANA.

But you are so quick.

GATTY.

Why, would it not make anyone mad to hear thee bewail
the loss of the country? Speak but one grave word more, 120

117. off] *Q1–2;* of *Q3.*

___

98. *point*] a piece of thread lace (made wholly with a needle) used
as a kerchief or the like.

and it shall be my daily prayers thou mayst have a
jealous husband, and then you'll have enough of it I
warrant you.

ARIANA.

It may be, if your tongue be not altogether so nimble, I
may comformable; but I hope you do not intend we shall 125
play such mad reaks as we did last summer?

GATTY.

'Slife, dost thou think we come here to be mewed up,
and take only the liberty of going from our chamber
to the dining room, and from the dining room to our
chamber again? And like a bird in a cage, with two 130
perches only, to hop up and down, up and down?

ARIANA.

Well, thou art a mad wench.

GATTY.

Wouldst thou never have us go to a play but with our
grave relations, never take the air but with our grave
relations? To feed their pride, and make the world 135
believe it is in their power to afford some gallant or
other a good bargain?

ARIANA.

But I am afraid we shall be known again.

GATTY.

Pish! The men were only acquainted with our vizards
and our petticoats, and they are wore out long since. 140
How I envy that sex! Well, we cannot plague 'em enough
when we have it in our power for those privileges which
custom has allowed 'em above us.

ARIANA.

The truth is, they can run and ramble, here and there,
and everywhere, and we poor fools rather think the 145
better of 'em.

122. and] *Q1; om. Q2–3.*

---

126. *reaks*] pranks.
127. *mewed up*] shut up, confined.
139. *vizards*] masks, usually of cloth, worn to conceal or disguise
the face.

GATTY.

From one playhouse, to the other playhouse, and if
they like neither the play nor the women, they seldom
stay any longer than the combing of their periwigs, or
a whisper or two with a friend. And then they cock their 150
caps, and out they strut again.

ARIANA.

But whatsoever we do, prithee now let us resolve to be
mighty honest.

GATTY.

There I agree with thee.

ARIANA.

And if we find the gallants like lawless subjects, who 155
the more their princes grant, the more they impudently
crave—

GATTY.

We'll become absolute tyrants, and deprive 'em of all
the privileges we gave 'em.

ARIANA.

Upon these conditions I am contented to trail a pike 160
under thee—march along, girl.   *Exeunt.*

---

160. *trail a pike*] a military exercise; figuratively, to take service
with, to follow the lead of.

ACT II

[II. i] *The Mulberry Garden. Enter* Courtall *and* Freeman.

COURTALL.

Was there ever a couple of fops better matched than
these two knights are?

FREEMAN.

They are harp and violin; Nature has so tuned 'em, as
if she intended they should always play the fool in
consort.   5

COURTALL.

Now is Sir Oliver secure, for he dares not go home
till he's quite drunk, and then he grows valiant, insults
and defies his sweet lady; for which with prayers and
tears he's forced to feign a bitter repentance the next
morning.   10

FREEMAN.

What do we here idling in the Mulberry Garden? Why
do not we make this visit then?

COURTALL.

Now art thou as mad upon this trail as if we were
upon a hot scent.

FREEMAN.

Since we know the bush, why do we not start the game?   15

COURTALL.

Gently, good Frank. First know that the laws of honor
prescribed in such nice cases will not allow me to carry
thee along with me; and next, hast thou so little wit to
think that a discreet lady that has had the experience of
so much human fraility, can have so good an opinion   20
of the constancy of her servant as to lead him into temptation?

0.1. *Mulberry Garden*] a garden of mulberry trees planted in 1609
by James I to encourage native silk manufacture. When the venture
failed, it became a place of public entertainment and one of the
fashionable resorts.

4–5. *in consort*] together, in accord.

FREEMAN.

Then we must not hope her ladyship should make us
acquainted with these gentlewomen.

COURTALL.

Thou mayst as reasonably expect that an old rook should   25
bring a young snap acquainted with his bubble; but
advantages may be hereafter made by my admission
into the family.

FREEMAN.

What is to be done then?

COURTALL.

Why, look you, thus I have contrived it. Sir Oliver, when   30
I began to grow resty, that he might incline me a little
more to drunkenness, in my ear discovered to me the humor of his dear friend Sir Joslin. He assured me that when
he was in that good-natured condition, to requite their
courtesy, he always carried the good company home with   35
him and recommended them to his kinswomen.

FREEMAN.

Very good!

COURTALL.

Now after the fresh air has breathed on us a while,
and expelled the vapors of the wine we have drunk,
thou shalt return to these two sots, whom we left at   40
the French House, according to our promise, and tell
'em I am a little stayed by some unlucky business, and
will be with 'em presently. Thou wilt find 'em tired
with long fight, weak and unable to observe their order.
Charge 'em briskly, and in a moment thou shalt rout   45
'em, and with little or no danger to thyself gain an
absolute victory.

FREEMAN.

Very well!

25, 26. *rook, snap*] a cheat, swindler, con man.
26. *bubble*] a dupe, gull, mark.
31. *resty*] restive.

COURTALL.

> In the meantime I will make my visit to the longing
> lady and order my business so handsomely that I will   50
> be with thee again immediately, to make an experiment
> of the good humor of Sir Joslin.

FREEMAN.

> Let's about it.

COURTALL.

> 'Tis yet too early. We must drill away a little time
> here, that my excuses may be more probable, and my   55
> persecution more tolerable.

> > *Enter* Ariana *and* Gatty *with vizards,*
> > *and pass nimbly over the stage.*

FREEMAN.

> Ha, ha. How wantonly they trip it! There is tempta-
> tion enough in their very gait to stir up the courage
> of an old alderman. Prithee let us follow 'em.

COURTALL.

> I have been so often baulked with these vizard-masks   60
> that I have at least a dozen times forsworn 'em. They
> are a most certain sign of an ill face, or what is worse,
> an old acquaintance.

FREEMAN.

> The truth is, nothing but some such weighty reason is
> able to make women deny themselves the pride they   65
> have to be seen.

COURTALL.

> The evening's fresh and pleasant, and yet there is but
> little company.

FREEMAN.

> Our course will be the better; these deer cannot herd.
> Come, come, man, let's follow.   70

COURTALL.

> I find it is a mere folly to forswear anything; it does

55. here] *Q1–2; om. Q3.*   71. forswear] *Q1;* swear *Q2–3.*

60. *vizard-masks*] women, frequently those of questionable reputation, who wear such masks.

but make the devil the more earnest in his temptation.

They go after the women.

Enter women again, and cross the stage.

ARIANA.

Now if these should prove two men-of-war that are
cruising here to watch for prizes.

GATTY.

Would they had courage enough to set upon us. I   75
long to be engaged.

ARIANA.

Look, look yonder. I protest they chase us.

GATTY.

Let us bear away then. If they be truly valiant they'll
quickly make more sail and board us.

*The women go out, and go about behind the scenes to the other
door.*

Enter Courtall *and* Freeman.

FREEMAN.

'Sdeath, how fleet they are! Whatsoever faults they have,   80
they cannot be broken-winded.

COURTALL.

Sure, by that little mincing step they should be country
fillies that have been breathed at Course-a-Park and
Barley-Break. We shall never reach 'em.

FREEMAN.

I'll follow directly. Do thou turn down the cross walk   85
and meet 'em.

72. but] *Q1–2;* put *Q3.*

---

74. *prizes*] ships captured at sea.

83. *breathed*] exercised.

83. *Course-a-Park*] a country game in which a girl called out a boy
to chase her *(OED).*

84. *Barley-Break*] an old country game originally played by six
persons, three of each sex, in couples. One couple, left in a middle
den, had to catch the others, who were allowed to separate when hard
pressed and thus to change partners, but had, when caught, to take
their turn as catchers *(OED).*

Enter the women, and after 'em Courtall *at the lower door, and* Freeman *at the upper on the contrary side.*

COURTALL.

By your leave, ladies—

GATTY.

I perceive you can make bold enough without it.

FREEMAN.

Your servant, ladies—

ARIANA.

Or any other ladies' that will give themselves the trouble   90
to entertain you.

FREEMAN.

'Slife, their tongues are as nimble as their heels.

COURTALL.

Can you have so little good nature to dash a couple
of bashful young men out of countenance, who came
out of pure love to tender you their service?   95

GATTY.

'Twere pity to baulk 'em, sister.

ARIANA.

Indeed methinks they look as if they never had been
slipped before.

FREEMAN.

Yes faith, we have had many a fair course in this
paddock, have been very well fleshed, and dare boldly 100
fasten.

They kiss their hands with a little force.

ARIANA.

Well, I am not the first unfortunate woman that has
been forced to give her hand where she never intends
to bestow her heart.

GATTY.

Now, do you think 'tis a bargain already?   105

---

98. *slipped*] released (as a greyhound or other dog, or a hawk) from
a leash or slip.

COURTALL.

Faith, would there were some lusty earnest given, for
fear we should unluckily break off again.

FREEMAN.

Are you so wild that you must be hooded thus?

COURTALL.

Fie, fie. Put off these scandals to all good faces.

GATTY.

For your reputations' sake we shall keep 'em on. 'Slife, 110
we should be taken for your relations if we durst shew
our faces with you thus publickly.

ARIANA.

And what a shame that would be to a couple of young
gallants! Methinks you should blush to think on't.

COURTALL.

These were pretty toys, invented, first, merely for the 115
good of us poor lovers to deceive the jealous and to
blind the malicious; but the proper use is so wickedly
perverted that it makes all honest men hate the fashion
mortally.

FREEMAN.

A good face is as seldom covered with a vizard-mask as 120
a good hat with an oiled case. And yet on my conscience,
you are both handsome.

COURTALL.

Do but remove 'em a little to satisfy a foolish scruple.

ARIANA.

This is a just punishment you have brought upon yourselves by that unpardonable sin of talking.   125

GATTY.

You can only brag now of your acquaintance with a
farendon gown and a piece of black velvet.

---

108. *hooded*] a reference to the leather covering used for hawks to
keep them quiet when not pursuing game; here referring more specifically to the vizard-masks.
127. *farendon*] variant spelling for "farandine," a kind of cloth made
partly of silk and partly of wool or hair.

COURTALL.

The truth is, there are some vain fellows whose loose
behavior of late has given great discouragement to the
honorable proceedings of all virtuous ladies.   130

FREEMAN.

But I hope you have more charity than to believe us
of the number of the wicked.

ARIANA.

There's not a man of you to be trusted.

GATTY.

What a shame is it to your whole sex, that a woman is
more fit to be a Privy Councilor than a young gallant 135
a lover.

COURTALL.

This is a pretty kind of fooling, ladies, for men that
are idle; but you must bid a little fairer, if you intend
to keep us from our serious business.

GATTY.

Truly you seem to be men of great employment that are 140
every moment rattling from the eating-houses to the
playhouses, from the playhouses to the Mulberry Garden,
that live in a perpetual hurry, and have little leisure
for such an idle entertainment.

COURTALL.

Now would not I see thy face for the world. If it should 145
but be half so good as thy humor, thou wouldst danger-
ously tempt me to dote upon thee, and forgetting all
shame, become constant.

FREEMAN.

I perceive, by your fooling here, that wit and good
humor may make a man in love with blackamoor. That 150
the devil should contrive it so that we should have
earnest business now.

COURTALL.

Would they would but be so kind to meet us here again
tomorrow.

145. not I] *Q1–2; I not Q3.*   146. but be] *Q1; be but Q2–3.*

GATTY.

You are full of business, and 'twould but take you off 155
of your employments.

ARIANA.

And we are very unwilling to have the sin to answer for
of ruining a couple of such hopeful young men.

FREEMAN.

Must we then despair?

ARIANA.

The ladies you are going to will not be so hardhearted. 160

COURTALL *(to* Freeman).

On my conscience, they love us, and begin to grow
jealous already.

FREEMAN [*to* Courtall].

Who knows but this may prove the luckier adventure of
the two?

COURTALL.

Come, come, we know you have a mind to meet us. We 165
cannot see you blush; speak it out boldly.

GATTY.

Will you swear then, not to visit any other women before that time?

ARIANA.

Not that we are jealous, but because we would not have
you tired with the impertinent conversation of our 170
sex, and come to us dull and out of humor.

COURTALL.

Invent an oath, and let it be so horrid 'twould make an
atheist start to hear it.

FREEMAN.

And I will swear it readily, that I will not so much as
speak to a woman, till I speak to you again.   175

GATTY.

But are you troubled with that foolish scruple of keeping
an oath?

FREEMAN.

Oh most religiously!

COURTALL.

And may we not enlarge our hopes upon a little better
acquaintance?   180

ARIANA.

You see all the freedom we allow.

GATTY.

It may be we may be intreated to hear a fiddle, or
mingle in a country dance, or so.

COURTALL.

Well! We are in too desperate a condition to stand upon
articles, and are resolved to yield on any terms.   185

FREEMAN.

Be sure you be punctual now!

ARIANA.

Will you be sure?

COURTALL.

Or else may we become a couple of credulous coxcombs,
and be jilted ever after. Your servants, ladies.   *Exit men.*

ARIANA.

I wonder what they think of us?   190

GATTY.

You may easily imagine; for they are not of a humor so
little in fashion to believe the best. I assure you the
most favorable opinion they can have is that we are
still a little wild, and stand in need of better manning.

ARIANA.

Prithee, dear girl, what dost think of 'em?   195

GATTY.

Faith, so well that I'm ashamed to tell thee.

ARIANA.

Would I had never seen 'em!

GATTY.

Ha! Is it come to that already?

ARIANA.

Prithee, let's walk a turn or two more, and talk of 'em.

---

185. *articles*] formal agreements.

GATTY.

Let us take care then we are not too particular in 200
their commendations, lest we should discover we en-
trench upon one another's inclinations, and so grow
quarrelsome.   *Exeunt.*

[II. ii]

Sir Oliver's lodgings. Enter Lady Cockwood *and* Sentry.

SENTRY.

Dear madam, do not afflict yourself thus unreasonably;
I dare lay my life it is not want of devotion, but opportunity that stays him.

LADY COCKWOOD.

Ingrateful man! To be so insensible of a lady's passion!

SENTRY.

If I thought he were so wicked, I should hate him   5
strangely. But, madam—

LADY COCKWOOD.

Do not speak one word in his behalf. I am resolved
to forget him. Perfidious mortal, to abuse so sweet an
opportunity!

SENTRY.

Hark, here is somebody coming upstairs.   10

LADY COCKWOOD.

Peace, he may yet redeem his honor.

Enter Courtall.

COURTALL.

Your humble servant, madam.

LADY COCKWOOD *(starting).*

Mr. Courtall, for Heaven's sake, how came you hither?

COURTALL.

Guided by my good fortune, madam—your servant, Mrs.
Sentry.   15

SENTRY.

Your humble servant, sir. I protest you made me start
too, to see you come in thus unexpectedly.

-31-

LADY COCKWOOD.

I did not imagine it could be known I was in town yet.

COURTALL.

Sir Oliver did me the favor to make me a visit, and dine
with me today, which brought me to the knowledge of   20
this happiness, madam. And as soon as I could possibly,
I got the freedom to come hither and enjoy it.

LADY COCKWOOD.

You have ever been extreme obliging, sir.

SENTRY *(aside)*.

'Tis a worthy gentleman. How punctual he is to my
directions.   25

LADY COCKWOOD.

Will you be pleased to repose, sir? Sentry, set some
chairs.   *Exit* Sentry.

COURTALL.

With much difficulty, madam, I broke out of my com-
pany, and was forced by the importunity of one Sir
Joslin Jolly, I think they call him, to engage my honor   30
I would return again immediately.

LADY COCKWOOD.

You must not so soon rob me of so sweet a satisfaction.

COURTALL.

No consideration, madam, could take me from you, but
that I know my stay at this time must needs endanger
your honor; and how often I have denied myself the   35
greatest satisfaction in the world to keep that unblemished you yourself can witness.

LADY COCKWOOD.

Indeed I have often had great trials of your generosity
in those many misfortunes that have attended our
innocent affections.   40

COURTALL.

Sir Oliver, madam, before I did perceive it, was got
near that pitch of drunkenness which makes him come
reeling home, and unmanfully insult over your ladyship. And how subject he is then to injure you with an

unjust suspicion, you have often told me, which makes   45
me careful not to be surprised here.

LADY COCKWOOD.

Repose yourself a little, but a little, dear sir. These
virtuous principles make you worthy to be trusted with
a lady's honor. Indeed Sir Oliver has his failings; yet I
protest, Mr. Courtall, I love him dearly, but cannot be   50
altogether unsensible of your generous passion.

COURTALL *(aside)*.

Aye, aye, I am a very passionate lover! [*To her.*] Indeed this escape has only given me leisure to look upon
my happiness.

LADY COCKWOOD.

Is my woman retired?   55

COURTALL.

Most dutifully, madam.

LADY COCKWOOD.

Then let me tell you, sir, yet we may make very good use
of it.

COURTALL *(aside)*.

Now am I going to be drawn in again.

LADY COCKWOOD.

If Sir Oliver be in that indecent condition you speak   60
of, tomorrow he will be very submissive, as it is meet for
so great a misdemeanor. Then can I, feigning a desperate discontent, take my own freedom without the least
suspicion.

COURTALL.

This is very luckily and obligingly thought on, madam.   65

LADY COCKWOOD.

Now if you will be pleased to make an assignation, sir.

COURTALL.

Tomorrow about ten a clock in the lower walk of the
New Exchange, out of which we can quickly pop into
my coach.

LADY COCKWOOD.

But I am still so pestered with my woman; I dare not   70
go without her. On my conscience she's very sincere, but

it is not good to trust our reputations too much to the
frailty of a servant.

COURTALL.

I will bring my chariot, madam; that will hold but two.

LADY COCKWOOD.

Oh most ingeniously imagined, dear sir! For by that   75
means I shall have a just excuse to give her leave to
see a relation, and bid her stay there till I call her.

COURTALL.

It grieves me much to leave you so soon, madam; but
I shall comfort myself with the thoughts of the happiness
you have made me hope for.   80

LADY COCKWOOD.

I wish it were in my power eternally to oblige you, dear
sir.

COURTALL.

Your humble servant, madam.

LADY COCKWOOD.

Your humble servant, sweet sir.   *Exit* Courtall.
Sentry—why Sentry—where are you?   85

Enter Sentry.

SENTRY.

Here, madam.

LADY COCKWOOD.

What a strange thing is this! Will you never take warn-
ing, but still be leaving me alone in these suspicious
occasions?

SENTRY.

I was but in the next room, madam.   90

LADY COCKWOOD.

What may Mr. Courtall think of my innocent inten-
sions? I protest if you serve me so again, I shall be
strangely angry. You should have more regard to your
lady's honor.

SENTRY [*aside*].

If I stay in the room, she will not speak kindly to me   95
in a week after; and if I go out, she always chides me
thus. This is a strange infirmity she has, but I must

bear with it; for on my conscience, custom has made it
so natural, she cannot help it.

LADY COCKWOOD.

Are my cousins come home yet?   100

SENTRY.

Not yet, madam.

LADY COCKWOOD.

Dost thou know whither they went this evening?

SENTRY.

I heard them say they would go take the air, madam.

LADY COCKWOOD.

Well, I see it is impossible with virtuous counsel to
reclaim them; truly they are so careless of their own, 105
I could wish Sir Joslin would remove 'em, for fear they
should bring an unjust imputation on my honor.

SENTRY.

Heavens forbid, madam!

Enter Ariana *and* Gatty.

LADY COCKWOOD.

Your servant, cousins.

ARIANA. GATTY.

Your servant, madam.   110

LADY COCKWOOD.

How have you spent the cool of the evening?

GATTY.

As the custom is, madam, breathing the fresh air in the
Park and Mulberry Garden.

LADY COCKWOOD.

Without the company of a relation, or some discreet
body to justify your reputations to the world—you are 115
young, and may be yet insensible of it, but this is a
strange censorious age, I assure you.

Noise of music without.

ARIANA.

Hark! What music's this?

GATTY.

I'll lay my life my uncle's drunk, and hath picked us

up a couple of worthy servants, and brought them home   120
with him in triumph.

Enter the Music playing, Sir Oliver *strutting and swaggering,*
Sir Joslin *singing, and dancing with* Mr. Courtall *and* Mr. Freeman *in each hand.* Gatty *and* Ariana, *seeing* Courtall *and* Freeman, *shriek and exeunt.*

SIR JOSLIN.

Hey-day! I told you they were a couple of skittish
fillies, but I never knew 'em boggle at a man before;
I'll fetch 'em again I warrant you, boys.   *Exit after them.*
FREEMAN (*to* Courtall).

These are the very self-same gowns and petticoats.   125
COURTALL.

Their surprise confirms us it must be them.
FREEMAN.

'Slife, we have betrayed ourselves very pleasantly.
COURTALL.

Now am I undone to all intents and purposes, for they
will innocently discover all to my lady, and she will
have no mercy.   130
SIR OLIVER.

Dan, dan, da ra, dan &c. *(Strutting.)* Avoid my presence; the very sight of that face makes me more impotent
than an eunuch.
LADY COCKWOOD (*offering to embrace him*).

Dear Sir Oliver!
SIR OLIVER.

Forbear your conjugal clippings. I will have a wench.   135
Thou shalt fetch me a wench, Sentry.
SENTRY.

Can you be so inhumane to my dear lady?
SIR OLIVER.

Peace, Envy, or I will have thee executed for petty treason, thy skin flayed off, stuffed, and hung up in my hall
in the country, as a terror to my whole family.   140
COURTALL.

What crime can deserve this horrid punishment?

SIR OLIVER.

I'll tell thee, Ned. 'Twas my fortune t'other day to have
an intrigue with a tinker's wife in the country, and this
malicious slut betrayed the very ditch where we used to
make our assignations to my lady.   145

FREEMAN.

She deserves your anger indeed, Sir Oliver. But be not
so unkind to your virtuous lady.

SIR OLIVER.

Thou dost not know her, Frank. I have had a design to
break her heart ever since the first month that I had
her, and 'tis so tough that I have not yet cracked one 150
string on't.

COURTALL.

You are too unmerciful, Sir Oliver.

SIR OLIVER.

Hang her, Ned. By wicked policy she would usurp my
empire, and in her heart is a very pharaoh; for every
night she's a-putting me upon making brick without 155
straw.

COURTALL.

I cannot see a virtuous lady so afflicted, without offering her some consolation. *(Aside to her.)* Dear madam,
is it not as I told you?

LADY COCKWOOD *(to* Courtall *aside).*

The fates could not have been more propitious, and I 160
shall not be wanting to the furthering of our mutual
happiness.

Enter Sir Joslin, *with* Ariana *and* Gatty *in each hand, dancing
and singing.*

CATCH

This is sly and pretty,
And this is wild and witty;
If either stayed   165
Till she died a maid,
I'faith 'twould be great pity.

SIR JOSLIN.

> Here they are boys, i'faith, and now little Joslin's a man
> of his word. Heuk! Sly-girl and Mad-cap, to 'em, to
> 'em, to 'em, boys, alou!   170
>
> *Flings 'em to* Courtall *and* Freeman, *who kiss their hands.*
> What's yonder, your lady in tears, Brother Cockwood?
> Come, come, I'll make up all breaches.   *He sings.*
> And we'll all be merry and frolick.
> Fie, fie, though man and wife are seldom in good humor
> alone, there are few want the discretion to dissemble 175
> it in company.

Sir Joslin, Sir Oliver, *and* Lady [Cockwood] *stand talking together.*

FREEMAN.

> I knew we should surprise you, ladies.

COURTALL.

> Faith, I thought this conjuring to be but a mere jest
> till now, and could not believe the astrological rascal had
> been so skilful.   180

FREEMAN.

> How exactly he described 'em, and how punctual he
> was in his directions to apprehend 'em!

GATTY.

> Then you have been with a conjurer, gentlemen.

COURTALL.

> You cannot blame us, ladies. The loss of our hearts was
> so considerable that it may well excuse the indirect 185
> means we took to find out the pretty thieves that stole
> 'em.

ARIANA.

> Did not I tell you what men of business these were,
> sister?

GATTY.

> I vow I innocently believed they had some pre-engage- 190
> ment to a scrivener or a surgeon, and wished 'em so well,
> that I am sorry to find 'em so perfidious.

FREEMAN.

> Why, we have kept our oaths, ladies.

ARIANA.

You are much beholding to Providence.

GATTY.

But we are more, sister; for had we once been deluded 195
into an opinion they had been faithful, who knows
into what inconveniences that error might have drawn
us?

COURTALL.

Why should you be so unreasonable, ladies, to expect
that from us, we should scarce have hoped for from 200
you? Fie, fie, the keeping of one's word is a thing below
the honor of a gentleman.

FREEMAN.

A poor shift! Fit only to uphold the reputation of a
paltry Citizen.

SIR JOSLIN.

Come, come, all will be well again, I warrant you lady. 205

LADY COCKWOOD.

These are insupportable injuries, but I will bear 'em
with an invincible patience, and tomorrow make him
dearly sensible how unworthy he has been.

SIR JOSLIN.

Tomorrow my Brother Cockwood will be another man—
So, boys, and how do you like the flesh and blood of the 210
Jollies?— Heuk, Sly-Girl—and Mad-cap, hey— Come,
come, you have heard them exercise their tongues a
while; now you shall see them ply their feet a little.
This is a clean-limbed wench, and has neither spavin,
splinter, nor wind-gall; tune her a jig, and play't roundly, 215
you shall see her bounce it away like a nimble frigate
before a fresh gale. Hey, methinks I see her under sail
already.   *Gatty dances a jig.*

Hey my little Mad-cap— Here's a girl of the true
breed of the Jollies, i'faith. But hark you, hark you 220

---

204. *Citizen*] literally a resident of the City of London, but by
extension, any merchant.

214–215. *spavin . . . wind-gall*] tumors found on the legs of horses.

a consultation, gentlemen— Bear up, Brother Cockwood, a little. What think you if we pack these idle
huswives to bed now, and retire into a room by ourselves,
and have a merry catch, and bottle or two of the best,
and perfect the good work we have so unanimously car- 225
ried on today?

SIR OLIVER.

A most admirable intrigue. Tan, dan, da, ra, dan. Come,
come, march to your several quarters. Go, we have sent
for a civil person or two, and are resolved to fornicate
in private.   230

LADY COCKWOOD.

This is a barbarous return of all my kindness.

FREEMAN. COURTALL.

Your humble servant, madam.

                         Exit Lady Cockwood *and* Sentry.

COURTALL.

Hark you! Hark you! Ladies, do not harbor too ill an
opinion of us, for faith, when you have had a little
more experience of the world, you'll find we are no 235
such abominable rascals.

GATTY.

We shall be so charitable to think no worse of you than
we do of all mankind for your sakes, only that you are
prejured, perfidious, inconstant, ingrateful.

FREEMAN.

Nay, nay, that's enough, in all conscience, ladies. And 240
now you are sensible what a shameful thing it is to
break one's word, I hope you'll be more careful to keep
yours tomorrow.

GATTY.

Invent an oath, and let it be so horrid—

COURTALL.

Nay, nay, it is too late for raillery, i'faith, ladies.   245

---

224. *catch*] a round, especially applied to rounds in which the words
are so arranged as to produce ludicrous effects, one singer catching at
the words of another.

GATTY. ARIANA.

Well, your servant then.

FREEMAN. COURTALL.

Your servant, ladies.   [*Exit* Ariana *and* Gatty.]

SIR OLIVER.

Now the enemy's marched out—

SIR JOSLIN.

Then the castle's our own, boys—hey!
          And here and there I had her,   250
          And everywhere I had her,
          Her toy was such, that every touch
          Would make a lover madder.

FREEMAN. COURTALL.

Hey, brave Sir Joslin!

SIR OLIVER.

Ah my dear little witty Joslin, let me hug thee.   255

SIR JOSLIN.

Strike up, you obstreperous rascals, and march along
before us.   *Exeunt singing and dancing.*

The end of the Second Act.

257.1. *The . . . Act.*] *Q1; om. Q2–3.*

ACT III

[III. i]
The New Exchange. Mrs. Trinket *sitting in a shop, people passing by as in the Exchange.*

TRINKET.

What d'ye buy? What d'ye lack, gentlemen? Gloves, ribbons, and essences; ribbons, gloves, and essences?

Enter Mr. Courtall.

Mr. Courtall! I thought you had a quarrel to the 'Change, and were resolved we should never see you here again.   5

COURTALL.

Your unkindness indeed, Mrs. Trinket, had been enough to make a man banish himself forever.

Enter Mrs. Gazette.

TRINKET.

Look you, yonder comes fine Mrs. Gazette; thither you intended your visit, I am sure.

GAZETTE.

Mr. Courtall! Your servant.   10

COURTALL.

Your servant, Mrs. Gazette.

GAZETTE.

This happiness was only meant to Mrs. Trinket. Had it not been my good fortune to pass by, I should have lost my share on't.

COURTALL.

This is too cruel, Mrs. Gazette, when all the unkindness   15
is on your side, to rally your servant thus.

GAZETTE.

I vow this tedious absence of yours made me believe you intended to try an experiment on my poor heart to discover that hidden secret, how long a despairing lover may languish without sight of the party.   20

COURTALL.

You are always very pleasant on this subject, Mrs. Gazette.

GAZETTE.

And have not you reason to be so too?

COURTALL.

Not that I know of.

GAZETTE.

Yes, you hear the good news.   25

COURTALL.

What good news?

GAZETTE.

How well this dissembling becomes you! But now I think better on't, it cannot concern you; you are more a gentleman than to have an amour last longer than an Easter Term with a country lady. And yet   30 there are some I see as well in the country as in the city, that have a pretty way of huswifing a lover, and can spin an intrigue out a great deal farther than others are willing to do.

COURTALL.

What pretty art have they, good Mrs. Gazette?   35

GAZETTE.

When tradesmen see themselves in an ill condition, and are afraid of breaking, can they do better than to take in a good substantial partner, to help to carry on their trading?

COURTALL.

Sure you have been at Riddle me, riddle me, lately;   40 you are so wondrous witty.

GAZETTE.

And yet I believe my Lady Cockwood is so haughty, she had rather give over the vanity of an intrigue than take

23. so too?] *Q1, 3*; be soo? *Q2*.   27. you!] *Q1;* you? *Q2–3*.

---

30. *Easter Term*] one of the four terms during which the law courts were in session.

37. *breaking*] becoming bankrupt.

40. *Riddle me, riddle me*] a riddle game.

in a couple of young handsome kinswomen to help to
maintain it.   45

COURTALL.

I knew it would out at last. Indeed it is the principle
of most good women that love gaming, when they begin
to grow a little out of play themselves, to make an interest in some young gamester or other, in hopes to rook
a favor now and then. But you are quite out in your   50
policy; my Lady Cockwood is none of these, I assure
you.— [*Talking privately to her.*] Hark you, Mrs.
Gazette, you must needs bestir yourself a little for me
this morning, or else Heaven have mercy on a poor
sinner.   55

GAZETTE.

I hope this wicked woman has no design upon your
body already. Alas! I pity your tender conscience.

COURTALL.

I have always made thee my confident, and now I come
to thee as to a faithful counselor.

GAZETTE.

State your case.   60

COURTALL.

Why, this ravenous kite is upon wing already, is fetch-
ing a little compass, and will be here within this half
hour to swoop me away.

GAZETTE.

And you would have me your scarecrow?

COURTALL.

Something of that there is in't. She is still your customer.   65

GAZETTE.

I have furnished her and the young ladies with a few
fashionable toys since they came to town, to keep 'em
in countenance at a play or in the Park.

COURTALL.

I would have thee go immediately to the young ladies,
and by some device or other entice 'em hither.   70

---

61. *kite*] a bird of prey.

GAZETTE.

I came just now from taking measure of 'em for a
couple of handkerchiefs.

COURTALL.

How unlucky's this!

GAZETTE.

They were calling for their hoods and scarfs, and are
coming hither to lay out a little money in ribbons and   75
essences. I have recommended them to Mrs. Trinket's
shop here.

COURTALL.

This falls out more luckily than what I had contrived
myself, or could have done. For here will they be busy
just before the door, where we have made our appoint-   80
ment. But if this long-winged devil should chance to
truss me before they come.

GAZETTE.

I will only step up and give some directions to my maid,
about a little business that is in haste, and come down
again and watch her; if you are snapped, I'll be with   85
you presently, and rescue you I warrant you, or at least
stay you till more company come. She dares not force
you away in my sight; she knows I am great with Sir
Oliver, and as malicious a devil as the best of 'em.
Your servant, sir.   *Exit* Gazette.   90

Enter Freeman.

COURTALL.

Freeman! 'Tis well you are come.

FREEMAN.

Well! What counter-plot? What hopes of disappointing
the old, and of seeing the young ladies? I am ready to
receive your orders.

COURTALL.

Faith, things are not so well contrived as I could have   95
wished 'em, and yet I hope by the help of Mrs. Gazette
to keep my word, Frank.

–45–

FREEMAN.

Nay, now I know what tool thou hast made choice of,
I make no question but the business will go well forward. But I am afraid this last unlucky business has 100
so distasted these young trouts, they will not be so
easily tickled as they might have been.

COURTALL.

Never fear it. Whatsoever women say, I am sure they
seldom think the worse of a man for running at all;
'tis a sign of youth and high mettle, and makes them 105
rather pique, who shall tame him. That which troubles
me most is, we have lost the hopes of variety, and a single
intrigue in love is as dull as a single plot in a play, and
will tire a lover worse than t'other does an audience.

FREEMAN.

We cannot be long without some underplots in this 110
town; let this be our main design, and if we are anything fortunate in our contrivance, we shall make it a
pleasant comedy.

COURTALL.

Leave all things to me, and hope the best. Be gone,
for I expect their coming immediately; walk a turn or 115
two above, or fool a while with pretty Mrs. Anvill,
and scent your eyebrows and perriwig with a little essence of oranges or jessamine; and when you see us
all together at Mrs. Gazette's shop, put in as it were by
chance. I protest yonder comes the old haggard; to your 120
post quickly. 'Sdeath, where's Gazette and these young
ladies now?   *Exit* Freeman.

Enter Lady Cockwood, *and* Sentry.

Oh madam, I have waited here at least an hour, and
time seems very tedious when it delays so great a happiness as you bring with you.   125

---

102. *tickled*] reference to a means of catching trout or other fish
by hand.
106. *pique*] competitive because of jealousy or envy.

LADY COCKWOOD.

I vow, sir, I did but stay to give Sir Oliver his due correction for those unseemly injuries he did me last night.
Is your coach ready?

COURTALL.

Yes, madam. But how will you dispose of your maid?

LADY COCKWOOD.

My maid! For Heaven's sake, what do you mean, sir? 130
Do I ever use to go abroad without her?

COURTALL.

'Tis upon no design, madam, I speak it, I assure you.
But my glass coach broke last night, and I was forced
to bring my chariot, which can hold but two.

LADY COCKWOOD.

Oh Heaven! You must excuse me, dear sir, for I shall 135
deny myself the sweetest recreations in the world rather
than yield to anything that may bring a blemish upon
my spotless honor.

Enter Gazette.

GAZETTE.

Your humble servant, madam. Your servant, Mr. Courtall.   ·   140

LADY COCKWOOD. COURTALL.

Your servant, Mrs. Gazette.

GAZETTE.

I am extreme glad to see your ladyship here; I intended
to send my maid to your lodgings this afternoon, madam,
to tell you I have a parcel of new lace come in, the
prettiest patterns that ever were seen. For I am very 145
desirous so good a customer as your ladyship should
see 'em first, and have your choice.

LADY COCKWOOD.

I am much beholding to you, Mrs. Gazette; I was newly
come into the Exchange, and intended to call at your
shop before I went home.   150

---

133. *glass coach*] a coach with glass windows, as distinguished from
curtain coaches whose windows were unglazed.

Enter Ariana *and* Gatty, Gazette *goes to 'em.*

COURTALL.

'Sdeath, here are your cousins too! Now there is no
hopes left for a poor unfortunate lover to comfort himself withal.

LADY COCKWOOD.

Will fate never be more propitious?

ARIANA. GATTY.

Your servant, madam.   155

LADY COCKWOOD.

I am newly come into the Exchange, and by chance met
with Mr. Courtall here, who will needs give himself
the trouble to play the gallant and wait upon me.

GATTY.

Does your ladyship come to buy?

LADY COCKWOOD.

A few trifles. Mrs. Gazette says she has a parcel of very 160
fine new laces; shall we go look upon 'em?

ARIANA.

We will only fancy a suit of knots or two at this shop,
and buy a little essence, and wait upon your ladyship
immediately.

GATTY.

Mrs. Gazette, you are skilled in the fashion, pray let 165
our choice have your approbation.

GAZETTE.

Most gladly, madam.

All go to the shop to look upon ware but Courtall *and* Lady
Cockwood.

152. hopes] *Q1;* hope *Q2–3.*   167. 1–2.] *Brett-Smith; in Q1–3,*
154. Will . . . propitious?] *Q1;*   *follows l. 166.*
om. Q2–3.

---

162. *suit of knots*] a group of bows of ribbon worn as an ornament
on a dress.

COURTALL.

'Sdeath, madam, if you had made no ceremony, but
stepped into the coach presently, we had escaped this
mischief.   170

LADY COCKWOOD.

My over-tenderness of my honor has blasted all my hopes
of happiness.

COURTALL.

To be thus unluckily surprised in the height of all our
expectation leaves me no patience.

LADY COCKWOOD.

Moderate your passion a little, sir, I may yet find out   175
a way.

COURTALL.

Oh 'tis impossible, madam; never think on't now you
have been seen with me. To leave 'em upon any pre-
tense will be so suspicious that my concern for your
honor will make me so feverish and disordered, that I   180
shall lose the taste of all the happiness you give me.

LADY COCKWOOD.

Methinks you are too scrupulous, heroic sir.

COURTALL.

Besides the concerns I have for you, madam, you know
what obligations I have to Sir Oliver, and what profes-
sions of friendship there are on both sides. And to be   185
thought perfidious and ingrateful, what an affliction
would that be to a generous spirit!

LADY COCKWOOD.

Must we then unfortunately part thus?

COURTALL.

Now I have better thought on't, that is not absolutely
necessary neither.   190

LADY COCKWOOD.

These words revive my dying joys; dear sir, go on.

COURTALL.

I will by and by, when I see it most convenient, beg the
favor of your ladyship, and your young kinswomen, to

175. sir,] *Q1–2;* sir? *Q3.*

---

accept of a treat and a fiddle; you make some little difficulty at first, but upon earnest persuasion comply, and   195
use your interest to make the young ladies do so too.
Your company will secure their reputations, and their
company take off from you all suspicion.

LADY COCKWOOD.

The natural inclination they have to be jigging will
make them very ready to comply. But what advantage   200
can this be to our happiness, dear sir?

COURTALL.

Why, first, madam, if the young ladies or Mrs. Gazette
have any doubts upon their surprising us together, our
joining company will clear 'em all; next, we shall have
some satisfaction in being an afternoon together, though   205
we enjoy not that full freedom we so passionately desire.

LADY COCKWOOD.

Very good, sir.

COURTALL.

But then lastly, madam, we gain an opportunity to
contrive another appointment tomorrow, which may
restore us unto all those joys we have been so unfortun-   210
ately disappointed of today.

LADY COCKWOOD.

This is a very prevailing argument indeed; but since
Sir Oliver believes I have conceived so desperate a sor-
row, 'tis fit we should keep this from his knowledge.

COURTALL.

Are the young ladies secret?   215

LADY COCKWOOD.

They have the good principles not to betray themselves,
I assure you.

COURTALL.

Then 'tis but going to a house that is not haunted by
the company, and we are secure; and now I think on't,
the Bear in Drury Lane is the fittest place for our pur-   220
pose.

194. a fiddle] *Q2–3;* a a fiddle *Q1.*

LADY COCKWOOD.

I know your honor, dear sir, and submit to your discretion.

To them Ariana, Gatty, *and* Gazette *from the shop.*

Have you gratified your fancies, cousins?

ARIANA.

We are ready to wait upon you, madam.   225

GATTY.

I never saw colors better mingled.

GAZETTE.

How lively they set off one another, and how they add
to the complexion!

LADY COCKWOOD.

Mr. Courtall, your most humble servant.

COURTALL.

Pray, madam, let me have the honor to wait upon you 230
and these young ladies till I see you in your coach.

LADY COCKWOOD.

Your friendship to Sir Oliver would engage you in an
unnecessary trouble.

ARIANA.

Let not an idle ceremony take you from your serious
business, good sir.   235

GATTY.

I should rather have expected to have seen you, sir,
walking in Westminster Hall, watching to make a match
at tennis, or waiting to dine with a Parliament man, than
to meet you in such an idle place as the Exchange is.

COURTALL.

Methinks, ladies, you are well acquainted with me upon 240
the first visit.

ARIANA.

We received your character before, you know, sir, in
the Mulberry Garden upon oath.

237–38. *walking . . . man*] At Westminster Hall, the seat of the law
courts, one might meet prominent people of London; an ambitious
young man might make valuable acquaintance there.

COURTALL *(aside)*.

'Sdeath, what shall I do? Now out comes all my roguery.

GATTY.

Yet I am apt to believe, sister, that was some malicious 245
fellow that wilfully perjured himself on purpose to make
us have an ill opinion of this gentlemen.

COURTALL.

Some rash men would be apt enough to enquire him
out, and cut his throat, ladies, but I heartily forgive him
whosoever he was; for on my conscience 'twas not so 250
much out of malice to me, as out of love to you he
did it.

GAZETTE.

He might imagine Mr. Courtall was his rival.

COURTALL.

Very likely, Mrs. Gazette.

LADY COCKWOOD.

Whosoever he was, he was an unworthy fellow I warrant 255
him; Mr. Courtall is known to be a person of worth
and honor.

ARIANA.

We took him for an idle fellow, madam, and gave but
very little credit to what he said.

COURTALL.

'Twas very obliging, lady, to believe nothing to the dis- 260
advantage of a stranger.— *(Aside.)* What a couple of
young devils are these!

LADY COCKWOOD.

Since you are willing to give yourself this trouble.

COURTALL.

I ought to do my duty, madam.

> *Exeunt all but* Ariana *and* Gatty.

ARIANA.

How he blushed, and hung down his head! 265

GATTY.

A little more had put him as much out of countenance,

261. S.D. *Aside*] Q3; *om.* Q1–2.

as a country clown is when he ventures to compliment
his attorney's daughter.   *They follow.*

[III. ii]
Sir Oliver's *dining room. Enter* Sir Joslin *and* Servant *severally.*

SIR JOSLIN.

Hey now old boy! where's my Brother Cockwood today?

SERVANT.

He desires to be in private, sir.

SIR JOSLIN.

Why? What's the matter, man?

SERVANT.

This is a day of humiliation, sir, with him for last
night's transgression.   5

SIR JOSLIN.

I have business of consequence to impart to him, and
must and will speak with him—So, ho! Brother Cockwood!

SIR OLIVER *(without).*

Who's that, my Brother Jolly?

SIR JOSLIN.

The same, the same, come away, boy.   10

SIR OLIVER *(without).*

For some secret reasons I desire to be in private, Brother.

SIR JOSLIN.

I have a design on foot as would draw Diogenes out of
his tub to follow it; therefore I say, come away, come
away.

SIR OLIVER *(entering in a nightgown and slippers).*

There is such a strange temptation in thy voice, never   15
stir.

SIR JOSLIN.

What, in thy gown and slippers yet! Why brother, I
have bespoke dinner, and engaged Mr. Rake-hell, the
little smart gentleman I have often promised thee to

III.ii] *In Q1 the scene-heading   to* SCENE II.
reads simply SCENE; *Q2–3 correct*

make thee acquainted withal, to bring a whole bevy of   20
damsels in sky, and pink, and flame-colored taffetas.
Come, come, dress thee quickly; there's to be Madam
Rampant, a girl that shines, and will drink at such a
rate, she's a mistress for Alexander, were he alive again.

SIR OLIVER.

How unluckily this falls out! Thomas, what clothes have   25
I to put on?

SERVANT.

None but your penitential suit, sir, all the rest are
secured.

SIR OLIVER.

Oh unspeakable misfortune! That I should be in disgrace with my lady now!   30

SIR JOSLIN.

Come, come, never talk of clothes. Put on anything; thou
hast a person and a mind will bear it out bravely.

SIR OLIVER.

Nay, I know my behavior will show I am a gentleman;
but yet the ladies will look scurvily upon me, brother.

SIR JOSLIN.

That's a jest i'faith! He that has *terra firma* in the   35
country, may appear in anything before 'em.

> For he that would have a wench kind,
> Ne'er smugs up himself like a ninny;
> But plainly tells her his mind,
> And tickles her first with a guinea.   40

Hey boy—

SIR OLIVER.

I vow thou hast such a bewitching way with thee!

SIR JOSLIN.

How lovely will the ladies look when they have a beer
glass in their hands!

32. mind] *Q3;* mine *Q1–2.*   41. Hey] *Q3;* Hay *Q1–2.*

---

38. *smugs*] smarten up one's appearance.
40. *guinea*] a coin, worth twenty-one shillings.

SIR OLIVER.

    I now have a huge mind to venture; but if this should   45
come to my lady's knowledge—

SIR JOSLIN.

    I have bespoke dinner at the Bear, the privatest place
in town. There will be no spies to betray us; if Thomas
be but secret, I dare warrant thee, Brother Cockwood.

SIR OLIVER.

    I have always found Thomas very faithful; but faith   50
'tis too unkind, considering how tenderly my lady loves
me.

SIR JOSLIN.

    Fie, fie, a man, and kept so much under correction by
a busk and a fan!

SIR OLIVER.

    Nay, I am in my nature as valiant as any man, when   55
once I set out; but i'faith I cannot but think how my
dear lady will be concerned when she comes home and
misses me.

SIR JOSLIN.

    A pox upon these qualms.

SIR OLIVER.

    Well, thou hast seduced me; but I shall look so unto-   60
wardly.

SIR JOSLIN.

    Again art thou at it? In, in, and make all the haste
that may be; Rake-hell and the ladies will be there
before us else.

SIR OLIVER.

    Well, thou art an errant devil—hey—for the ladies,   65
Brother Jolly.

SIR JOSLIN.

    Hey for the ladies, Brother Cockwood.

                    Exit singing, "For he that would," &c.

---

54. *a busk and a fan*] a woman; a busk is a piece of stiffening ma-
terial for corsets.

[III. iii]   *The Bear.*

[SERVANT] *(without).*

    Ho Francis, Humphrey, show a room there!

Enter Courtall, Freeman, Lady Cockwood, Ariana, Gatty, *and* Sentry.

COURTALL.

    Pray, madam, be not so full of apprehension; there is no fear that this should come to Sir Oliver's knowledge.

LADY COCKWOOD.

    I were ruined if it should, sir! Dear, how I tremble! I never was in one of these houses before.   5

SENTRY *(aside).*

    This is a bait for the young ladies to swallow; she has been in most of the eating-houses about town, to my knowledge.

COURTALL.

    Oh Francis!

Enter Waiter.

WAITER.

    Your worship's welcome, sir; but I must needs desire   10 you to walk into the next room, for this is bespoke.

LADY COCKWOOD.

    Mr. Courtall, did not you say this place was private?

COURTALL.

    I warrant you, madam. What company dines here, Francis?

WAITER.

    A couple of country knights, Sir Joslin Jolly and Sir   15 Oliver Cockwood, very honest gentlemen.

LADY COCKWOOD.

    Combination to undo me!

COURTALL.

    Peace, madam, or you'll betray yourself to the waiter.

LADY COCKWOOD.

    I am distracted! Sentry, did not I command thee to se- cure all Sir Oliver's clothes, and leave nothing for him   20

to put on but his penitential suit, that I might be sure
he could not stir abroad today?

SENTRY.

I obeyed you in everything, madam; but I have often
told you this Sir Joslin is a wicked seducer.

ARIANA.

If my uncle sees us, sister, what will he think of us?   25

GATTY.

We come but to wait upon her ladyship.

FREEMAN.

You need not fear; you chickens are secure under the
wings of that old hen.

COURTALL.

Is there to be nobody, Francis, but Sir Oliver and Sir
Joslin?   30

WAITER.

Faith, sir, I was enjoined to secrecy; but you have an
absolute power over me. Coming lately out of the country, where there is but little variety, they have a design
to solace themselves with a fresh girl or two, as I understand the business.   *Exit* Waiter.   35

LADY COCKWOOD.

Oh Sentry! Sir Oliver disloyal! My misfortunes come too
thick upon me.

COURTALL *(aside)*.

Now is she afraid of being disappointed on all hands.

LADY COCKWOOD.

I know not what to do, Mr. Courtall; I would not be
surprised here myself, and yet I would prevent Sir Oliver   40
from prosecuting his wicked and perfidious intentions.

ARIANA [*to* Gatty].

Now shall we have admirable sport, what with her fear
and jealousy.

GATTY [*to* Ariana].

I lay my life she routs the wenches.

Enter Waiter.

WAITER.

> I must needs desire you to step into the next room; 45
> Sir Joslin and Sir Oliver are below already.

LADY COCKWOOD.

> I have not power to move a foot.

FREEMAN.

> We will consider what is to be done within, madam.

COURTALL.

> Pray, madam, come; I have a design in my head which
> shall secure you, surprise Sir Oliver, and free you from 50
> all your fears.

LADY COCKWOOD.

> It cannot be, sir.

COURTALL.

> Never fear it. Francis, you may own Mr. Freeman and I
> are in house, if they ask for us; but not a word of these
> ladies, as you tender the wearing of your ears.   *Exeunt.* 55

Enter Sir Joslin, Sir Oliver, *and* Waiter.

SIR JOSLIN.

Come, Brother Cockwood, prithee be brisk.

SIR OLIVER.

I shall disgrace myself forever, brother.

SIR JOSLIN.

> Pox upon care. Never droop like cock in moulting
> time; thou art spark enough, in all conscience.

SIR OLIVER.

But my heart begins to fail me when I think of my lady. 60

SIR JOSLIN.

What, more qualms yet?

SIR OLIVER.

> Well, I will be courageous. But it is not necessary these
> strangers should know this is my penitential suit, brother.

SIR JOSLIN.

> They shall not, they shall not. Hark you old boy, is
> the meat provided? Is the wine and ice come? And are 65
> melodious rascals at hand I spoke for?

WAITER.

Everything will be in a readiness, sir.

SIR JOSLIN.

If Mr. Rake-hell, with a coachful or two of vizard-masks
and silk petticoats call at the door, usher 'em up to the
place of execution.   *Exit* Waiter. 70

Enter Rake-hell.

SIR JOSLIN.

Ho, here's my little Rake-hell come! Brother Cockwood,
let me commend this ingenious gentleman to your acquaintance; he is a knight of the industry, has many
admirable qualities, I assure you.

SIR OLIVER.

I am very glad, sir, of this opportunity to know you. 75

RAKE-HELL.

I am happy, sir, if you esteem me your servant. Hark
you, Sir Joslin, is this Sir Oliver Cockwood in earnest?

SIR JOSLIN.

In very good earnest I assure you; he is a little fantas-
tical now and then, and dresses himself up in an odd
fashion. But that's all one among friends, my little Rake- 80
hell.

SIR OLIVER.

Where are the damsels you talked of, Brother Jolly? I
hope Mr. Rake-hell has not forgot 'em.

RAKE-HELL.

They are arming for the rencounter.

SIR JOSLIN.

What, tricking and trimming?   85

RAKE-HELL.

Even so, and will be here immediately.

SIR OLIVER.

They need not make themselves so full of temptation;
my Brother Jolly and I can be wicked enough without
it.

67. a] *Q1–2; om. Q3.*

84. *rencounter*] encounter.

SIR JOSLIN.

> The truth is, my little Rake-hell, we are both mighty   90
> men at arms, and thou shalt see us charge anon to the
> terror of the ladies.

RAKE-HELL.

> Methinks that dress, Sir Oliver, is a little too rustical for
> a man of your capacity.

SIR OLIVER.

> I have an odd humor, sir, now and then; but I have   95
> the wherewithal at home to be as spruce as any man.

RAKE-HELL.

> Your periwig is too scandalous, Sir Oliver; your black
> cap and border is never wore but by a fiddler or a waiter.

SIR JOSLIN.

> Prithee, my little Rake-hell, do not put my Brother
> Cockwood out of conceit of himself; methinks your   100
> calot is a pretty ornament, and makes a man look both
> polite and politic.

RAKE-HELL.

> I will allow you, 'tis a grave ware, and fit for men of
> business, that are every moment bending of their brows
> and scratching of their heads; every project would claw   105
> out another periwig. But a lover had better appear be-
> fore his mistress with a bald pate. 'Twill make the ladies
> apprehend a savor, stop their noses, and avoid you. 'Slife,
> love in a cap is more ridiculous than love in a tub, or
> love in a pipkin.   110

SIR OLIVER.

> I must confess your whole head is now in fashion; but
> there was a time when your calot was not so despicable.

RAKE-HELL.

> Here's a peruke, sir.

---

101. *calot*] usually a skullcap; here probably a skullcap with a fringe of hair. See l. 98.

109–110. *love in a tub . . . pipkin*.] *Love in a Tub* is, of course, the sub-title of Etherege's first play; *love in a pipkin* seems to be only a playful variation of the title.

SIR OLIVER.

A very good one.

RAKE-HELL.

A very good one? 'Tis the best in England. Pray, Sir 115
Joslin, take him in your hand, and draw a comb through
him; there is not such another frizz in Europe.

SIR JOSLIN.

'Tis a very fine one indeed.

RAKE-HELL.

Pray, Sir Oliver, do me the favor to grace it on your
head a little.   120

SIR OLIVER.

To oblige you, sir.

RAKE-HELL.

You never wore anything became you half so well in
all your life before.

SIR JOSLIN.

Why, you never saw him in your life before.

RAKE-HELL.

That's all one, sir, I know 'tis impossible. Here's a 125
beaver, Sir Oliver, feel him; for fineness, substance, and
for fashion, the court of France never saw a better; I have
bred him but a fortnight, and have him at command
already. Clap him on boldly. Never hat took the fore-
cock and the hind-cock at one motion so naturally.   130

SIR OLIVER.

I think you have a mind to make a spark of me before
I see the ladies.

RAKE-HELL.

Now you have the mien of a true cavalier, and with one
look may make a lady kind, and a hector humble. And
since I named a hector, here's a sword, sir. Sa, sa, sa, 135

---

126. *beaver*] a low-crowned, broad-brimmed hat of beaver fur.
135. *hector*] a swaggering fellow; in this period applied frequently
to a set of disorderly young men who infested the streets of London.

try him. Sir Joslin, put him to't, cut through the staple, run him through the door, beat him to the hilts. If he breaks, you shall have liberty to break my pate, and pay me never a groat of the ten for't.

SIR JOSLIN.

'Tis a very pretty weapon, indeed, sir.   140

RAKE-HELL.

The hilt is true French-wrought, and *doree* by the best workman in France. This sword and this castor, with an embroidered button and loop, which I have to vary him upon occasion, were sent me out of France for a token by my elder brother, that went over with a handsome 145 equipage, to take the pleasure of this champaign.

SIR OLIVER.

Have you a mind to sell these things, sir?

RAKE-HELL.

That is below a gentleman; yet if a person of honor or a particular friend, such as I esteem you, Sir Oliver, take at any time a fancy to a band, a cravat, a velvet coat, 150 a vest, a ring, a flageolet, or any other little toy I have about me, I am good-natured, and may be easily persuaded to play the fool upon good terms.

Enter Freeman.

SIR JOSLIN.

Worthy Mr. Freeman!

SIR OLIVER.

Honest Frank, how camest thou to find us out, man? 155

136–137. *cut . . . hilts*] These tests reveal the quality of a sword by exhibiting its cutting ability, strength, and durability. The *staple* is probably a reference to the iron fastening of a door.

139. *groat . . . ten*] A groat was an English coin, originally equal to four pence, which ceased to be minted after 1662. Here the phrase seems to be equivalent to "not a penny of the purchase price."

141. *doree*] gilded.

142. *castor*] a hat, the beaver of 1. 126.

143. *button and loop*] part of the trim of the hat which helped it to hold the desired cock.

151. *flageolet*] a small wind instrument.

FREEMAN.

By mere chance, sir; Ned Courtall is without writing a
letter, and I came in to know whether you had any particular engagements, gentlemen.

SIR OLIVER.

We resolved to be in private; but you are men without
exception.   160

FREEMAN.

Methinks you intended to be in private indeed, Sir
Oliver. 'Sdeath, what disguise have you got on? Are you
grown grave since last night, and come to sin incognito?

SIR OLIVER.

Hark you in your ear, Frank. This is my habit of humiliation, which I always put on the next day after I have 165
transgressed, the better to make my pacification with
my incensed lady.

FREEMAN.

Ha, ha, ha—

RAKE-HELL.

Mr. Freeman, your most humble servant, sir.

FREEMAN.

Oh my little dapper officer! Are you here?   170

SIR JOSLIN.

Ha, Mr. Freeman, we have bespoke all the jovial entertainment that a merry wag can wish for: good meat,
good wine, and a wholesome wench or two for the
digestion. We shall have Madam Rampant, the glory of
the town, the brightest she that shines, or else my little 175
Rake-hell is not a man of his word, sir.

RAKE-HELL.

I warrant you she comes, Sir Joslin.

[SIR JOSLIN] (sings).

> And if she comes, she shall not 'scape,
> If twenty pounds will win her;
> Her very eye commits a rape,   180
> 'Tis such a tempting sinner.

173. two] Q2–3; two; Q1.

---

175. she] slang for prostitute.

Enter Courtall.

COURTALL.

Well said, Sir Joslin. I see you hold up still, and bate
not an ace of your good humor.

SIR JOSLIN.

Noble Mr. Courtall!

COURTALL.

Bless me, Sir Oliver, what, are you going to act a droll? 185
How the people would throng about you, if you were but
mounted on a few deal-boards in Convent Garden now!

SIR OLIVER.

Hark you, Ned, this is the badge of my lady's indignation for my last night's offense; do not insult over a
poor sober man in affliction. 190

COURTALL.

Come, come, send home for your clothes; I hear you
are to have ladies, and you are not to learn at these
years how absolutely necessary a rich vest and a peruke
are to a man that aims at their favors.

SIR OLIVER.

A pox on't, Ned. My lady's gone abroad in a damned 195
jealous melancholy humor, and has commanded her
woman to secure 'em.

COURTALL.

Under lock and key?

SIR OLIVER.

Aye, aye, man. 'Tis usual in these cases, out of pure
love in hopes to reclaim me, and to keep me from doing 200
myself an injury by drinking two days together.

COURTALL.

What a loving lady 'tis.

SIR OLIVER.

There are sots that would think themselves happy in
such a lady, Ned; but to a true-bred gentleman all
lawful solace is abomination. 205

---

185. *droll*] a comic or farcial composition.
187. *deal-boards*] planks of pine or fir wood; here a stage.

RAKE-HELL.

Mr. Courtall, your most humble servant, sir.

COURTALL.

Oh! my little knight of the industry. I am glad to see
you in such good company.

FREEMAN.

Courtall, hark you, are the masking habits which you
sent to borrow at the playhouse come yet?   210

COURTALL.

Yes, and the ladies are almost dressed. This design
will add much to our mirth, and give us the benefit
of their meat, wine, and music for our entertainment.

FREEMAN.

'Twas luckily thought of.

Music [*within*].

SIR OLIVER.

Hark, the music comes.   215

SIR JOSLIN.

Hey, boys—let 'em enter, let 'em enter.

Enter Waiter.

WAITER.

An't please your worships, there is a mask of ladies
without that desire to have the freedom to come in and
dance.

SIR JOSLIN.

Hey! boys—   220

SIR OLIVER.

Did you bid 'em come *en masquerade,* Mr. Rake-hell?

RAKE-HELL.

No; but Rampant is a mad wench. She was half a
dozen times a-mumming in private company last Shrovetide, and I lay my life she has put 'em upon this frolic.

---

223. *mumming*] the action of disguising oneself; specifically, of taking part in a mummer's play.

223–224. *Shrovetide*] a time of merriment and carnival immediately
preceding Lent.

COURTALL.

They are mettled girls, I warrant them, Sir Joslin, let 225
'em be what they will.

SIR JOSLIN.

Let 'em enter, let 'em enter, ha boys—

*Enter Music and the ladies in an antick, and then they take
out: my* Lady Cockwood, Sir Oliver; *the young ladies,* Courtall
and Freeman; *and* Sentry, Sir Joslin; *and dance a set dance.*

SIR OLIVER.

Oh my little rogue! Have I got thee? How I will turn
and wind, and feague thy body!

SIR JOSLIN.

Mettle on all sides, mettle on all sides, i'faith; how 230
swimmingly would this pretty little ambling filly carry
a man of my body!   *Sings.*

    She's so bony and brisk,
    How she'd curvet and frisk,
    If a man were once mounted upon her!   235
    Let me have but a leap
    Where 'tis wholesome and cheap,
    And a fig for your person of honor.

SIR OLIVER.

'Tis true, little Joslin, i'faith.

COURTALL.

They have warmed us, Sir Oliver.   240

SIR OLIVER.

Now am I as rampant as a lion, Ned, and could love

234. curvet] *Q3;* carvet *Q1-2.*

---

225. *mettled*] spirited.

227.1. *antick*] a grotesque pageant or theatrical representation;
sometimes refers to the anti-masque. See Enid Welsford, *The Court
Masque* (New York, 1962).

227.1-2. *take out*] a technical phrase for the action at the latter
part of some masques where the mummers invite members of the audience to join them in a dance.

229. *feague*] to get the best of.

234. *curvet*] a leaping, frisking motion.

as vigorously as a seaman that is newly landed after an
East India voyage.

COURTALL.

Take my advice, Sir Oliver. Do not in your rage deprive yourself of your only hope of an accommodation 245
with your lady.

SIR OLIVER.

I had rather have a perpetual civil war than purchase
peace at such a dishonorable rate. A poor fiddler, after
he has been three days persecuted at a country wedding,
takes more delight in scraping upon his old squeaking 250
fiddle than I do in fumbling on that domestic instrument
of mine.

COURTALL.

Be not so bitter, Sir Oliver, on your own dear lady.

SIR OLIVER.

I was married to her when I was young, Ned, with a
design to be baulked, as they tie whelps to the bell- 255
wether; where I have been so butted, 'twere enough
to fright me, were I not pure mettle, from ever running
at sheep again.

CCURTALL.

That's no sure rule, Sir Oliver; for a wife's a dish, of
which if a man once surfeit, he shall have a better 260
stomach to all others ever after.

SIR OLIVER.

What a shape is here, Ned! So exact and tempting,
'twould persuade a man to be an implicit sinner, and
take her face upon credit.

SIR JOSLIN.

Come, Brother Cockwood, let us get 'em to lay aside 265
these masking fopperies, and then we'll league 'em in
earnest. Give us a bottle, waiter.

247. than] *Q3;* then *Q1–2.*   255–256. bellwether] *Q3* (bell-
251. than] *Q3;* then *Q1–2.*   wether); bell-weather *Q1–2.*
                                        259. rule,] *Q1, 3;* rule; *Q2.*

255–256. *tie . . . bellwether*] the practice of tying young dogs to the
lead sheep in order to break them of bothering the sheep.

FREEMAN.

Not before dinner, good Sir Joslin.

SIR OLIVER.

Lady, though I have out of drollery put myself into
this contemptible dress at present, I am a gentleman, 270
and a man of courage, as you shall find anon by my
brisk behavior.

RAKE-HELL.

Sir Joslin! Sir Oliver! These are none of our ladies.
They are just come to the door in a coach, and have
sent for me down to wait upon 'em up to you.   275

SIR JOSLIN.

Hey—boys, more game, more game! Fetch 'em up, fetch
'em up.

SIR OLIVER.

Why, what a day of sport will here be, Ned!

Exit Rake-hell.

SIR JOSLIN.

They shall all have fair play, boys.

SIR OLIVER.

And we will match ourselves, and make a prize on't, 280
Ned Courtall and I, against Frank Freeman and you,
Brother Jolly, and Rake-hell shall be judge for gloves
and silk stockings, to be bestowed as the conqueror shall
fancy.

SIR JOSLIN.

Agreed, agreed, agreed.   285

COURTALL. FREEMAN.

A match, a match.

SIR OLIVER.

Hey, boys!

Lady Cockwood *counterfeits a fit.*

SENTRY *(pulling off her mask).*

Oh Heavens! my dear lady! Help, help!

SIR OLIVER.

What's here? Sentry and my lady! 'Sdeath, what a condition am I in now, Brother Jolly! You have brought me 290

into this praemunire. For Heaven's sake run down
quickly, and send the rogue and whores away. Help,
help! oh help! dear madam, sweet lady!

    Exit Sir Joslin. Sir Oliver *kneels down by her.*

SENTRY.

Oh she's gone, she's gone!

FREEMAN.

Give her more air.   295

COURTALL.

Fetch a glass of cold water, Freeman.

SIR OLIVER.

Dear madam, speak, sweet madam, speak.

SENTRY.

Out upon thee for a vile hypocrite! Thou art the wicked
author of all this; who but such a reprobate, such an
obdurate sinner as thou art, could go about to abuse so 300
sweet a lady?

SIR OLIVER.

Dear Sentry, do not stab me with thy words, but stab
me with thy bodkin rather, that I may here die a sacri-
fice at her feet for all my disloyal actions.

SENTRY.

No, live, live, to be a reproach and a shame to all re- 305
bellious husbands. Ah, that she had but my heart!
But thou hast bewitched her affections. Thou shouldst
then dearly smart for this abominable treason.

GATTY.

So, now she begins to come to herself.

ARIANA.

Set her more upright, and bend her a little forward. 310

LADY COCKWOOD.

Unfortunate woman! Let me go, why do you hold me?
Would I had a dagger at my heart, to punish it for loving that ungrateful man.

297. sweet madam, speak.] sweet madam speak *Q1–2; om. Q3.*

---

291. *praemunire*] a legal term, here used figuratively to mean a
scrape or difficulty.

SIR OLIVER.

Dear madam, were I but worthy of your pity and belief.

LADY COCKWOOD.

Peace, peace, perfidious man, I am too tame and foolish. 315
Were I every day at the plays, the Park, and Mulberry
Garden, with a kind look secretly to indulge the unlawful passion of some young gallant; or did I associate
myself with the gaming madams, and were every afternoon at my Lady Briefe's and my Lady Meanwell's at 320
ombre and quebas, pretending ill luck to borrow money
of a friend, and then pretending good luck to excuse
the plenty to a husband, my suspicious demeanor had
deserved this. But I who out of a scrupulous tenderness
to my honor, and to comply with thy base jealously, have 325
denied myself all those blameless recreations which a
virtuous lady might enjoy, to be thus inhumanely re-
viled in my own person, and thus unreasonably robbed
and abused in thine too!

COURTALL.

Sure she will take up anon, or crack her mind, or else 330
the devil's in't.

LADY COCKWOOD.

Do not stay and torment me with thy sight. Go, grace-
less wretch, follow thy treacherous resolutions, do, and
waste that poor stock of comfort which I should have
at home, upon those your ravenous cormorants below. 335
I feel my passion begin to swell again.

She has a little fit again.

COURTALL [*aside*].

Now will she get an absolute dominion over him, and
all this will be my plague in the end.

SIR OLIVER *(running up and down)*.

Ned Courtall, Frank Freeman, Cousin Ariana, and dear

---

321. *ombre*] a card game played by three persons with a special
deck; very popular at the time.

321. *quebas*] according to the *OED*, some kind of game, probably a
card game.

330. *take up*] stop.

Cousin Gatty, for Heaven's sake join all, and moderate 340
her passion. Ah Sentry! Forebear thy unjust reproaches,
take pity on thy master! Thou hast a great influence
over her, and I have always been mindful of thy favors.

SENTRY.

You do not deserve the least compassion, nor would I
speak a good word for you, but that I know for all this, 345
'twill be acceptable to my poor lady. Dear madam, do
but look up a little. Sir Oliver lies at your feet an
humble penitent.

ARIANA.

How bitterly he weeps! How sadly he sighs!

GATTY.

I dare say he counterfeited his sin, and is real in his 350
repentance.

COURTALL.

Compose yourself a little, pray, madam; all this was mere
raillery, a way of talk, which Sir Oliver, being well bred,
has learned among the gay people of the town.

FREEMAN.

If you did but know, madam, what an odious thing 355
it is to be thought to love a wife in good company, you
would easily forgive him.

LADY COCKWOOD.

No, no. 'Twas the mild correction which I gave him for
his insolent behavior last night that has encouraged
him again thus to insult over my affections.   360

COURTALL.

Come, come, Sir Oliver. Out with your bosom-secret,
and clear all things to your lady. Is it not as we have
said?

SIR OLIVER.

Or may I never have the happiness to be in her good
grace again. And as for the harlots, dear madam, here 365
is Ned Courtall and Frank Freeman, that have often
seen me in company of the wicked. Let 'em speak if they
ever knew me tempted to a disloyal action in their lives.

COURTALL.

On my conscience, madam, I may more safely swear that
Sir Oliver has been constant to your ladyship than that   370
a girl of twelve years old has her maidenhead this warm
and ripening age.

Enter Sir Joslin.

SIR OLIVER.

Here's my Brother Jolly too can witness the loyalty of my
heart, and that I did not intend any treasonable practice
against your ladyship in the least.   375

SIR JOSLIN.

Unless feaguing 'em with a beer glass be included in
the statute. Come, Mr. Courtall, to satisfy my lady, and
put her in a little good humor, let us sing the catch I
taught you yesterday that was made by a country vicar
on my Brother Cockwood and me.   380

They sing.

Love and wenching are toys,
Fit to please beardless boys,
They're sports we hate worse than a Leaguer;
When we visit a miss,
We still brag how we kiss,   385
But 'tis with a bottle we feague her.

Come, come, madam, let all things be forgot. Dinner
is ready, the cloth is laid in the next room; let us in and
be merry. There was no harm meant as I am true little
Joslin.   390

LADY COCKWOOD.

Sir Oliver knows I can't be angry with him, though he
plays the naughty man thus. But why, my dear, would
y'expose yourself in this ridiculous habit, to the censure
of both our honors?

370. than] *Q3;* then *Q1–2.*   383. than] *Q3;* then *Q1–2.*

---

383. *Leaguer*] a signer of the Solemn League and Covenant (1643),
i.e., a Puritan.

384. *miss*] a prostitute.

SIR OLIVER.

    Indeed I was to blame to be over-persuaded. I intended 395
    dutifully to retire into the pantry, and there civily to
    divert myself at backgammon with the butler.

SIR JOSLIN.

    Faith, I must ev'n own, the fault was mine. I enticed
    him hither, lady.

SIR OLIVER.

    How the devil, Ned, came they to find us out here?   400

COURTALL.

    No bloodhound draws so sure as a jealous woman.

SIR OLIVER.

    I am afraid Thomas has been unfaithful. Prithee, Ned,
    speak to my lady, that there my be a perfect understand-
    ing between us, and that Sentry may be sent home for
    my clothes that I may no longer wear the marks of her 405
    displeasure.

COURTALL.

    Let me, alone, Sir Oliver. *(He goes to my* Lady Cock-
    wood.) How do you find yourself, madam, after this
    violent passion?

LADY COCKWOOD.

    This has been a lucky adventure, Mr. Courtall. I am 410
    now absolute mistress of my own conduct for a time.

COURTALL.

    Then shall I be a happy man, madam. I knew this
    would be the consequence of all, and yet I could not
    forbear the project.

SIR OLIVER *(to* Sir Joslin).

    How didst thou shuffle away Rake-hell and the ladies, 415
    brother?

SIR JOSLIN.

    I have appointed 'em to meet us at six a clock at the
    new Spring Garden.

SIR OLIVER.

    Then will we yet, in spite of the stars that have crossed
    us, be in conjunction with Madam Rampant, brother. 420

COURTALL.

    Come, gentlemen. Dinner is on the table.

SIR JOSLIN.

    Ha! Sly-girl and Mad-cap, I'll enter you, i'faith. Since
    you have found the way to the Bear, I'll feague you.

Sings.

            When we visit a miss,
            We still brag how we kiss;   425
            But 'tis with a bottle we feague her.

Exeunt singing.

ACT IV

A dining room. Enter Lady Cockwood.

LADY COCKWOOD.

A lady cannot be too jealous of her servant's love, this
faithless and inconstant age. His amorous carriage to
that prating girl today, though he pretends it was to
blind Sir Oliver, I fear will prove a certain sign of his
revolted heart. The letters I have counterfeited in these   5
girls' name will clear all; if he accept of that appointment, and refuses mine, I need not any longer doubt.

Enter Sentry.

Sentry, have the letters and message been delivered as
I directed?

SENTRY.

Punctually, madam. I knew they were to be found at   10
the latter end of a play. I sent a porter first with the
letter to Mr. Courtall, who was at the King's House.
He sent for him out by the doorkeeper, and delivered
it into his own hands.

LADY COCKWOOD.

Did you keep on your vizard, that the fellow might not   15
know how to describe you?

SENTRY.

I did, madam.

LADY COCKWOOD.

And how did he receive it?

SENTRY.

Like a traitor to all goodness, with all the signs of joy
imaginable.   20

LADY COCKWOOD.

Be not angry, Sentry. 'Tis as my heart wished it. What
did you do with the letter to Mr. Freeman? For I thought

---

12. *King's House*] the theater in which the King's Company acted;
at this time the Theatre Royal near Drury Lane.

fit to deceive 'em both, to make my policy less suspicious
to Courtall.

SENTRY.

The porter found him at the Duke's House, madam, and   25
delivered it with like care.

LADY COCKWOOD.

Very well.

SENTRY.

After the letters were delivered, madam, I went myself
to the playhouse, and sent in for Mr. Courtall, who came
out to me immediately. I told him your ladyship pre-   30
sented your humble service to him, and that Sir Oliver
was going into the City with Sir Joslin, to visit his
Brother Cockwood, and that it would add much more
to your ladyship's happiness if he would be pleased
to meet you in Gray's Inn Walks this lovely evening.   35

LADY COCKWOOD.

And how did he entertain the motion?

SENTRY.

Bless me! I tremble still to think upon it! I could not
have imagined he had been so wicked. He counterfeited
the greatest passion, railed at his fate, and swore a
thousand horrid oaths, that since he came into the play-   40
house he had notice of a business that concerned both
his honor and fortune; and that he was an undone man
if he did not go about it presently; prayed me to desire
your ladyship to excuse him this evening, and that tomorrow he would be wholly at your devotion.   45

LADY COCKWOOD.

Ha, ha, ha! He little thinks how much he has obliged me.

SENTRY.

I had much ado to forbear upbraiding him with his
ingratitude to your ladyship.

---

25. *Duke's House*] the theater in which the Duke's Company acted;
at this time the theater was in Lincoln's Inn Fields. On February 6,
1667/68, *She Would If She Could* was first performed there.

32. *City*] the small, central section of London; adminstratively the
City of London; see also II.ii. 206.

LADY COCKWOOD.

Poor Sentry! Be not concerned for me. I have conquered
my affection, and thou shalt find it is not jealousy has   50
been my counselor in this. Go, let our hoods and masks
be ready that I may surprise Courtall and make the best
advantage of this lucky opportunity.

SENTRY.

I obey you, madam.   *Exit* Sentry.

LADY COCKWOOD.

How am I filled with indignation! To find my person   55
and my passion both despised, and what is more, so
much precious time fooled away in fruitless expectation.
I would poison my face, so I might be revenged on this
ingrateful villain.

Enter Sir Oliver.

SIR OLIVER.

My dearest!   60

LADY COCKWOOD.

My dearest dear! Prithee do not into the City tonight.

SIR OLIVER.

My Brother Jolly is gone before, and I am to call him
at Counselor Trott's chamber in the Temple.

LADY COCKWOOD.

Well, if you did but know the fear I have upon me when
you are absent, you would not seek occasions to be   65
from me thus.

SIR OLIVER.

Let me comfort thee with a kiss. What shouldst thou
be afraid of?

LADY COCKWOOD.

I cannot but believe that every woman that sees thee
must be in love with thee, as I am. Do not blame my   70
jealousy.

SIR OLIVER.

I protest I would refuse a countess rather than abuse
thee, poor heart.

55. indignation!] *Q1–2;* indignation? *Q3*

LADY COCKWOOD.

    And then you are so desperate upon the least occasion.
I should have acquainted you else with something that   75
concerns your honor.

SIR OLIVER.

    My honor! You ought in duty to do it.

LADY COCKWOOD.

    Nay, I knew how passionate you would be presently.
Therefore you shall never know it.

SIR OLIVER.

    Do not leave me in doubt. I shall suspect everyone I look   80
upon. I will kill a Common Councilman or two before
I come back, if you do not tell me.

LADY COCKWOOD.

    Dear, how I tremble! Will you promise me you will not
quarrel then? If you tender my life and happiness I am
sure you will not.   85

SIR OLIVER.

    I will bear anything rather than be an enemy to thy
quiet, my dear.

LADY COCKWOOD.

    I could wish Mr. Courtall a man of better principles,
because I know you love him, my dear.

SIR OLIVER.

    Why, what has he done?   90

LADY COCKWOOD.

    I always treated him with great respects, out of my regard
to your friendship. But he, like an impudent man as he is,
today misconstruing my civility, in most unseemly
language, made a foul attempt upon my honor.

SIR OLIVER.

    Death, and Hell, and Furies! I will have my pumps and   95
long sword.

86. than] *Q3;* then *Q1–2.*   95. Furies!] *Q3;* Furies, *Q1–2.*

    81. *Common Councilman*] a member of the King's Common Council,
as distinct from the Privy Council.
    95. *pumps*] light shoes worn where freedom of movement was re-
quired.

LADY COCKWOOD.

Oh, I shall faint! Did not you promise me you would
not be so rash?

SIR OLIVER.

Well, I will not kill him, for fear of murdering thee, my
dear.   100

LADY COCKWOOD.

You may decline your friendship, and by your coldness
give him no encouragement to visit our family.

SIR OLIVER.

I think thy advice the best for this once indeed; for it is
not fit to publish such business. But if he should be ever
tempting or attempting, let me know it, prithee, my dear. 105

LADY COCKWOOD.

If you moderate yourself according to my directions
now, I shall never conceal anything from you that may
increase your just opinion of my conjugal fidelity.

SIR OLIVER.

Was ever man blessed with such a virtuous lady!
(Aside). Yet cannot I forbear going a-ranging again. 110
Now must I to the Spring Garden to meet my Brother
Jolly and Madam Rampant.

LADY COCKWOOD.

Prithee, be so good to think how melancholy I spend
my time here. For I have joy in no company but thine,
and let that bring thee home a little sooner.   115

SIR OLIVER.

Thou hast been so kind in this discovery that I am
loath to leave thee.

LADY COCKWOOD.

I wish you had not been engaged so far.

SIR OLIVER.

Aye, that's it. Farewell, my virtuous dear.   *Exit* Sir Oliver.

LADY COCKWOOD.

Farewell, my dearest dear. I know he has not courage 120

---

116. *Spring Garden*] a reference to the new Spring Garden or Vauxhall, sometimes called the new Spring Garden (see ll. 129–130) to distinguish it from the old Spring Garden at Whitehall.

enough to question Courtall. But this will make him hate him, increase his confidence of me, and justify my banishing that false fellow our house. It is not fit a man that has abused my love should come hither and pry into my actions. Besides, this will make his access 125 more difficult to that wanton baggage.

Enter Ariana *and* Gatty *with their hoods and masks.*

Whither are you going, cousins?

GATTY.

To take the air upon the water, madam.

ARIANA.

And for variety, to walk a turn or two in the new Spring Garden. 130

LADY COCKWOOD.

I heard you were gone abroad with Mr. Courtall and Mr. Freeman.

GATTY.

For Heaven's sake, why should your ladyship have such an ill opinion of us?

LADY COCKWOOD.

The truth is, before I saw you, I believed it merely 135 the vanity of that prating man. Mr. Courtall told Mrs. Gazette this morning that you were so well acquainted already that you would meet him and Mr. Freeman any-where, and that you had promised 'em to receive and make appointment by letters. 140

GATTY.

Oh impudent man!

ARIANA.

Now you see the consequence, sister, of our rambling. They have raised this false story from our innocent fooling with 'em in the Mulberry Garden last night.

GATTY.

I could almost forswear every speaking to a man again. 145

---

128. *take . . . water*] to go for a ride on the river, a popular London recreation.

LADY COCKWOOD.

Was Mr. Courtall in the Mulberry Garden last night?

ARIANA.

Yes, madam.

LADY COCKWOOD.

And did he speak to you?

GATTY.

There passed a little harmless raillery betwixt us. But
you amaze me, madam.   150

ARIANA.

I could not imagine any man could be thus unworthy.

LADY COCKWOOD.

He has quite lost my good opinion too. In duty to Sir
Oliver, I have hitherto showed him some countenance.
But I shall hate him hereafter for your sakes. But I
detain you from your recreations, cousins.   155

GATTY.

We are very much obliged to your ladyship for this
timely notice.

ARIANA. GATTY.

Your servant, madam.   *Exit* Ariana *and* Gatty.

LADY COCKWOOD.

Your servant, cousins— In the Mulberry Garden last
night! When I sat languishing and vainly expecting him 160
at home. This has incensed me so that I could kill
him. I am glad these girls are gone to the Spring Garden;
it helps my design. The letters I have counterfeited
have appointed Courtall and Freeman to meet them
there; they will produce 'em, and confirm all I have   165
said. I will daily poison these girls with such lies as
shall make their quarrel to Courtall irreconcilable, and
render Freeman only suspected; for I would not have
him thought equally guilty. He secretly began to make
an address to me at the Bear, and this breach shall give 170
him an opportunity to pursue it.

Enter Sentry.

SENTRY.

Here are your things, madam.

LADY COCKWOOD.

That's well. Oh Sentry! I shall once more be happy.
For now Mr. Courtall has given me an occasion that I
may without ingratitude check his unlawful passion, and 175
free myself from the trouble of an intrigue that gives
me every day such fearful apprehensions of my honor.

Exit Lady Cockwood *and* Sentry.

[IV.ii]

New Spring Garden. Enter Sir Joslin, Rake-hell, *and* Waiter.

WAITER.

Will you be pleased to walk into an arbor, gentlemen?

SIR JOSLIN.

By and by, good sir.

RAKE-HELL.

I wonder Sir Oliver is not come yet.

SIR JOSLIN.

Nay, he will not fail I warrant thee, boy; but what's the
matter with thy nose, my little Rake-hell?   5

RAKE-HELL.

A foolish accident. Jesting at the Fleece this afternoon,
I mistook my man a little; a dull rogue that could not
understand raillery made a sudden repartee with a
quart pot, Sir Joslin.

SIR JOSLIN.

Why didst not thou stick him to the wall, my little   10
Rake-hell?

RAKE-HELL.

The truth is, Sir Joslin, he deserved it. But look you,
in case of a doubtful wound, I am unwilling to give my
friends too often the trouble to bail me; and if it should
be mortal, you know a younger brother has not where-   15
withal to rebate the edge of a witness and mollify the
hearts of a jury.

---

6. *Fleece*] a common name for taverns in London.

SIR JOSLIN.

This is very prudently considered indeed.

RAKE-HELL.

'Tis time to be wise, sir. My courage has almost run
me out of a considerable annuity. When I lived first   20
about this town, I agreed with a surgeon for twenty
pounds a quarter to cure me of all the knocks, bruises,
and green wounds I should receive, and in one-half
year the poor fellow begged me to be released of his
bargain, and swore I would undo him else in lint and   25
balsam.

Enter Sir Oliver.

SIR JOSLIN.

Ho! Here's my Brother Cockwood come.

SIR OLIVER.

Aye, Brother Jolly. I have kept my word, you see. But
'tis a barbarous thing to abuse my lady. I have had
such a proof of her virtue; I will tell thee all anon.   30
But where's Madam Rampant, and the rest of the ladies,
Mr. Rake-hell?

RAKE-HELL.

Faith, sir, being disappointed at noon, they were unwilling any more to set a certainty at hazard. 'Tis term-
time, and they have severally betook themselves, some to   35
their chamber practice, and others to the places of public
pleading.

SIR OLIVER.

Faith, Brother Jolly, let us ev'n go into an arbor, and
then feague Mr. Rake-hell.

SIR JOSLIN.

With all my heart. Would we had Madam Rampant.   40

Sings.

> She's as frolic and free
> As her lovers dare be,
> Never awed by a foolish punctilio;

---

23. *green wounds*] recent, unhealed wounds.

   She'll not start from her place,
   Though thou nam'st a black ace,   45
   And will drink a beer glass to spudilio.
Hey, boys! Come, come, come! Let's in, and delay our
sport no longer.

   Exit singing, "She'll not start from her," &c.

  Enter Courtall *and* Freeman *severally.*

COURTALL.

 Freeman!

FREEMAN.

 Courtall, what the devil's the matter with thee? I have   50
observed thee prying up and down the walks like a
Citizen's wife that has dropped her holiday pocket-
handkercher.

COURTALL.

 What unlucky devil has brought thee hither?

FREEMAN.

 I believe a better-natured devil then yours, Courtall,   55
if a leveret be better meat than an old puss that has
been coursed by most of the young fellows of her country. I am not working my brain for a counter-plot;
a disappointment is not my business.

COURTALL.

 You are mistaken, Freeman. Prithee be gone and leave   60
me the garden to myself, or I shall grow as testy as
an old fowler that is put by his shoot after he has crept
half a mile upon his belly.

FREEMAN.

 Prithee be thou gone, or I shall take it as unkindly
as a chemist would if thou shouldst kick down his lim-   65
beck in the very minute that he looked for projection.

52. holiday] *Q2–3;* holy-day *Q1.*

---

 46. *spudilio*] variant spelling of spadile, the name of the ace of
spades in ombre and quadrille.
 65–66. *limbeck*] variant spelling for alembic; an apparatus formerly
used in distilling.
 66. *projection*] the final stage in transmuting metal to gold or silver
through the use of the philosopher's stone.

COURTALL.

Come, come, you must yield, Freeman. Your business
cannot be of such consequence as mine.

FREEMAN.

If ever thou hadst a business of such consequence in
thy life as mine is, I will condescend to be made incap- 70
able of affairs presently.

COURTALL.

Why, I have an appointment made me, man, without my
seeking, by a woman for whom I would have mortgaged
my whole estate to have her abroad but to break a
cheese cake.   75

FREEMAN.

And I have an appointment made me without my seeking, too, by such a she, that I will break the whole ten
commandments, rather then disappoint her of her breaking one.

COURTALL.

Come, you do but jest, Freeman; a forsaken mistress   80
could not be more malicious then thou art. Prithee
be gone.

FREEMAN.

Prithee do thou be gone.

COURTALL.

'Sdeath! The sight of thee will scare my woman forever.

FREEMAN.

'Sdeath! The sight of thee will make my woman believe 85
me the falsest villain breathing.

COURTALL.

We shall stand fooling till we are both undone, and
I know not how to help it.

FREEMAN.

Let us proceed honestly like friends, discover the truth
of things to one another, and if we cannot reconcile   90
our business, we will draw cuts and part fairly.

COURTALL.

I do not like that way; for talk is only allowable at the
latter end of an intrigue, and should never be used

at the beginning of an amour, for fear of frighting
a young lady from her good intentions. Yet I care not   95
though I read the letter, but I will conceal the name.

FREEMAN.

I have a letter too, and am content to do the same.

COURTALL *(reads)*.

Sir, in sending you this letter, I proceed against the
modesty of our sex—

FREEMAN.

'Sdeath, this begins just like my letter.   100

COURTALL.

Do read on then.

FREEMAN *(reads)*.

But let not the good opinion I have conceived of you
make you too severe in your censuring of me—

COURTALL.

Word for word.

FREEMAN.

Now do you read again.   105

COURTALL *(reads)*.

If you give yourself the trouble to be walking in the
new Spring Garden this evening, I will meet you there,
and tell you a secret, which I have reason to fear, because it comes to your knowledge by my means, will
make you hate your humble servant.   110

FREEMAN.

Verbatim my letter, hey-day!

COURTALL.

I hope the name is not the same too.

FREEMAN.

If it be, we are finely jilted, faith.

COURTALL.

I long to be undeceived. Prithee do thou show first,
Freeman.   115

FREEMAN.

No—but both together, if you will.

110. make you] *Q3;* you make *Q1–2.*

COURTALL.

Agreed.

FREEMAN.

Ariana.

COURTALL.

Gatty. Ha, ha, ha.

FREEMAN.

The little rogues are masculine in their proceedings, 120
and have made one another confidents in their love.

COURTALL.

But I do not like this altogether so well, Frank; I wish
they had appointed us several places. For though 'tis
evident they have trusted one another with the bargain,
no woman ever seals before witness. 125

FREEMAN.

Prithee how didst thou escape the snares of the old
devil this afternoon?

COURTALL.

With much ado. Sentry had set me; if her ladyship
had got me into her clutches, there had been no getting
off without a rescue, or paying down the money; for 130
she always arrests upon execution.

FREEMAN.

You made a handsome lie to her woman.

COURTALL.

For all this, I know she's angry. For she thinks nothing
a just excuse in these cases, though it were to save the
forfeit of a man's estate or reprieve the life of her own 135
natural brother.

FREEMAN.

Faith, thou hast not done altogether like a gentleman
with her. Thou shouldst fast thyself up to a stomach
now and then to oblige her. If there were nothing in
it but the hearty welcome, methinks 'twere enough to 140
make thee bear sometimes with the homeliness of the
fare.

COURTALL.

I know not what I might do in a camp where there were

no other woman; but I shall hardly in this town, where
there is such plenty, forbear good meat to get myself 145
an appetite to horseflesh.

FREEMAN.

This is rather an aversion in thee, than any real fault in
the woman. If this lucky business had not fallen out,
I intended with your good leave to have outbid you for
her ladyship's favor. 150

COURTALL.

I should never have consented to that, Frank. Though
I am a little resty at present, I am not such a jade but
I should strain if another rid against me. I have ere
now liked nothing in a woman that I have loved in
spite only, because another had a mind to her. 155

FREEMAN.

Yonder are a couple of vizards tripping towards us.

COURTALL.

'Tis they, i'faith.

FREEMAN.

We need not divide since they come together.

COURTALL.

I was a little afraid when we compared letters they had
put a trick upon us; but now I am confirmed they are 160
mighty honest.

Enter Ariana *and* Gatty.

ARIANA.

We cannot avoid 'em.

GATTY.

Let us dissemble our knowledge of their business a
little, and then take 'em down in the height of their
assurance. 165

COURTALL. FREEMAN.

Your servant, ladies.

ARIANA.

I perceive it is as impossible, gentlemen, to walk with-

147. than] *Q3;* then *Q1–2.*

---

out you as without our shadows; never were poor women
so haunted by the ghosts of their self-murdered lovers.

GATTY.

If it should be our good fortunes to have you in love 170
with us, we will take care you shall not grow desperate,
and leave the world in an ill humor.

ARIANA.

If you should, certainly your ghosts would be very
malicious.

COURTALL.

'Twere pity you should have your curtains drawn in 175
the dead of the night, and your pleasing slumbers interrupted by anything but flesh and blood, ladies.

FREEMAN.

Shall we walk a turn?

ARIANA.

By yourselves, if you please.

GATTY.

Our company may put a constraint upon you. For I 180
find you daily hover about these gardens as a kite does
about a back-side watching an opportunity to catch
up the poultry.

ARIANA.

Woe be to the daughter or wife of some merchant-tailor
or poor felt-maker now; for you seldom row to Fox- 185
hall without some such plot against the City.

FREEMAN.

You wrong us, ladies. Our business has happily succeeded, since we have the honor to wait upon you.

GATTY.

You could not expect to see us here.

COURTALL.

Your true lover, madam, when he misses his mistress, 190
is as restless as a spaniel that has lost his master; he

---

182. *back-side*] the back part of a house or the yard in back of a
house.
185–186. *Fox-hall*] i.e., Vauxhall. See IV.i.111, Spring Garden.

ranges up and down the plays, the Park, and all the
gardens, and never stays long but where he has the happiness to see her.

GATTY.

I suppose your mistress, Mr. Courtall, is always the last 195
woman you are acquainted with.

COURTALL.

Do not think, madam, I have that false measure of my
acquaintance which poets have of their verses, always to
think the last best, though I esteem you so, in justice
to your merit.   200

GATTY.

Or if you do not love her best, you always love to talk
of her most; as a barren coxcomb that wants discourse
is ever entertaining company out of the last book he
read in.

COURTALL.

Now you accuse me most unjustly, madam. Who the devil 205
that has common sense will go a-birding with a clack
in his cap?

ARIANA.

Nay, we do not blame you, gentlemen; everyone in
their way. A huntsman talks of his dogs, a falconer
of his hawks, a jockey of his horse, and a gallant of his 210
mistress.

GATTY.

Without the allowance of this vanity, an amour would
soon grow as dull as matrimony.

COURTALL.

Whatsoever you say, ladies, I cannot believe you think
us men of such abominable principles.   215

FREEMAN.

For my part, I have ever held it as ingrateful to boast
of the favors of a mistress as to deny the courtesies
of a friend.

208. blame you,] *Q1–2;* blame, *Q3.*

---

206. *clack*] a noisemaking instrument; a rattle worked by the wind
to scare off birds.

COURTALL.

A friend that bravely ventures his life in the field to
serve me, deserves but equally with a mistress that kindly 220
exposes her honor to oblige me, especially when she
does it as generously too, and with as little ceremony.

FREEMAN.

And I would no more betray the honor of such a woman,
than I would the life of a man that should rob on purpose to supply me. 225

GATTY.

We believe you men of honor, and know it is below
you to talk of any woman that deserves it.

ARIANA.

You are so generous, you seldom insult after a victory.

GATTY.

And so vain, that you always triumph before it.

COURTALL.

'Sdeath! What's the meaning of all this? 230

GATTY.

Though you find us so kind, Mr. Courtall, pray do not
tell Mrs. Gazette tomorrow that we came hither on purpose this evening to meet you.

COURTALL.

I would as soon print it, and see a fellow to post it up
with the playbills. 235

GATTY.

You have reposed a great deal of confidence in her,
for all you pretend this ill opinion of her secrecy now.

COURTALL.

I never trusted her with the name of a mistress that I
should be jealous of, if I saw her receive fruit, and go
out of the playhouse with a stranger. 240

GATTY.

For aught as I see, we are infinitely obliged to you, sir.

COURTALL.

'Tis impossible to be insensible of so much goodness,
madam.

GATTY.

What goodness, pray sir?

COURTALL.

Come, come, give over this raillery.   245

GATTY.

You are so ridiculously unworthy, that 'twere a folly
to reprove you with a serious look.

COURTALL.

On my conscience, your heart begins to fail you now
we are coming to the point, as a young fellow's that
never was in the field before.   250

GATTY.

You begin to amaze me.

COURTALL.

Since you yourself sent the challenge, you must not in
honor fly off now.

GATTY.

Challenge! Oh Heavens! This confirms all. Were I a
man, I would kill thee for the injuries thou hast al- 255
ready done me.

FREEMAN (to Ariana).

Let not your suspicion of my unkindness make you thus
scrupulous; was ever city ill treated that surrendered
without assault or summons?

ARIANA.

Dear sister, what ill spirit brought us hither? I never 260
met with so much impudence in my life.

COURTALL (aside).

Hey jilts! They are as good at it already as the old
one i'faith.

FREEMAN.

Come, ladies, you have exercised your wit enough. You
would not venture letters of such consequence for a 265
jest only.

GATTY.

Letters! Bless me, what will this come to?

COURTALL.

> To that none of us shall have cause to repent I hope,
> madam.

ARIANA.

> Let us fly 'em, sister. They are devils and not men; they 270
> could never be so malicious else.

Enter Lady Cockwood *and* Sentry.

LADY COCKWOOD.

> Your servant, cousins.

COURTALL *(starting)*.

> Ho my Lady Cockwood! My ears are grown an inch
> already.

ARIANA.

> My lady! She'll think this an appointment, sister.   275

FREEMAN.

> This is Madam Machiavil, I suspect, Courtall.

COURTALL.

> Nay, 'tis her plot doubtless. Now am I as much out of
> countenance as I should be if Sir Oliver should take
> me making bold with her ladyship.

LADY COCKWOOD.

> Do not let me discompose you; I can walk alone, cousins. 280

GATTY.

> Are you so uncharitable, madam, to think we have any
> business with 'em?

ARIANA.

> It has been our ill fortune to meet 'em here, and noth-
> ing could be so lucky as your coming, madam, to free
> us from 'em.   285

GATTY.

> They have abused us in the grossest manner.

ARIANA.

> Counterfeited letters under our hands.

LADY COCKWOOD.

> Never trouble yourselves, cousins; I have heard this

---

273. *ears . . . inch*] apparently because he thinks he has been made
to appear a fool or jackass.

is a common practice with such unworthy men. Did
they not threaten to divulge them and defame you to 290
to the world?

GATTY.

We cannot believe they intend anything less, madam.

LADY COCKWOOD.

Doubtless they had such a mean opinion of your wit
and honor that they thought to fright you to a base
compliance with their wicked purposes.   295

ARIANA.

I hate the very sight of 'em.

GATTY.

I could almost wish myself a disease to breathe infec-
tion upon 'em.

COURTALL.

Very pretty! We have carried our designs very luckily
against these young ladies.   300

FREEMAN.

We have lost their good opinion forever.

LADY COCKWOOD.

I know not whether their folly or their impudence be
greater. They are not worth your anger; they are only
fit to be laughed at, and despised.

COURTALL [aside].

A very fine old devil this!   305

LADY COCKWOOD.

Mr. Freeman, this is not like a gentleman, to affront
a couple of young ladies thus; but I cannot blame
you so much. You are in a manner a stranger to our
family. But I wonder how that base man can look me
in the face, considering how civilly he has been treated 310
at our house.

COURTALL.

The truth is, madam, I am a rascal; but I fear you have
contributed to the making me so. Be not as unmerciful
as the devil is to a poor sinner.

299. pretty!] *Q1–2;* pretty? *Q3.*

SENTRY.

Did you ever see the like? Never trust me, if he has 315
not the confidence to make my virtuous lady accessary
to his wickedness.

LADY COCKWOOD.

Aye Sentry! 'Tis a miracle if my honor escapes, considering the access which his greatness with Sir Oliver
has given him daily to me.   320

FREEMAN.

Faith, ladies, we did not counterfeit these letters. We
are abused as well as you.

COURTALL.

I received mine from a porter at the King's Playhouse,
and I will show it you that you may see if you know
the hand.   325

LADY COCKWOOD.

Sentry, are you sure they never saw any of your writing?

COURTALL.

'Sdeath! I am so discomposed, I know not where I have
put it.

SENTRY.

Oh madam! Now I remember myself, Mrs. Gatty helped
me once to indite a letter to my sweetheart.   330

LADY COCKWOOD.

Forgetful wench! Then I am undone.

COURTALL.

Oh here it is— Hey, who's here?

As he has the letter in hand, enter Sir Joslin, Sir Oliver, *and*
Rake-hell, *all drunk, with music. They sing.*

She's no mistress of mine
That drinks not her wine,
Or frowns at my friends' drinking motions;   335
If my heart thou wouldst gain,
Drink thy bottle of champagne.
'Twill serve thee for paint and love-potions.

SIR OLIVER.

Who's here? Courtall, in my lady's company! I'll dispatch him presently. Help me, Brother Jolly.*He draws.* 340

LADY COCKWOOD.

    For Heaven's sake, Sir Oliver!

COURTALL *(drawing)*.

    What do you mean, sir?

SIR OLIVER.

    I'll teach you more manners than to make your attempts
on my lady, sir.

LADY COCKWOOD. SENTRY.

    Oh! Murder! Murder!   *They shriek.* 345

LADY COCKWOOD.

    Save my dear Sir Oliver. Oh my dear Sir Oliver!

*The young ladies shriek and run out. They all draw to part 'em,
they fight off the stage. She shrieks and runs out [with Sentry].*

343. than] *Q3;* then *Q1–2.*   346. Oh my] *Q2–3;* Oh my. *Q1.*

ACT V

Sir Oliver's dining room. Enter Lady Cockwood, *table, and carpet.*

LADY COCKWOOD.

I did not think he had been so desperate in his drink;
if they had killed one another, I had then been revenged, and freed from all my fears.

Enter Sentry.

Sentry, your carelessness and forgetfulness some time
or other will undo me. Had not Sir Oliver and Sir   5
Joslin came so luckily into the Garden, the letters had
been discovered, and my honor left to the mercy of a
false man and two young fleering girls. Did you speak
to Mr. Freeman unperceived in the hurry?

SENTRY.

I did, madam, and he promised me to disengage himself   10
as soon as possibly he could, and wait upon your ladyship with all secrecy.

LADY COCKWOOD.

I have some reason to believe him a man of honor.

SENTRY.

Methinks indeed his very look, madam, speaks him to
be much more a gentleman than Mr. Courtall. But I was 15
unwilling before now to let your ladyship know my
opinion, for fear of offending your inclinations.

LADY COCKWOOD.

I hope by his means to get these letters into my own
hands, and so prevent the inconveniences they may
bring upon my honor.   20

SENTRY.

I wonder, madam, what should be Sir Oliver's quarrel
to Mr. Courtall.

15. than] *Q3;* then *Q1–2.*

0.1. *table, and carpet*] This appears to be part of the stage direction,
indicating that a table and tablecloth (carpet) are to be brought onto
the stage by servants before the action begins.

8. *fleering*] jibing, jeering, sneering.

LADY COCKWOOD.

You know how apt he is to be suspicious in his drink.
'Tis very likely he thought Mr. Courtall betrayed him
at the Bear today.   25

SENTRY.

Pray Heaven he be not jealous of your ladyship, finding
you abroad so unexpectedly. If he be, we shall have a
sad hand of him when he comes home, madam.

LADY COCKWOOD.

I should have apprehended it much myself, Sentry, if
his drunkenness had not unadvisedly engaged him in his   30
quarrel. As soon as he grows a little sober, I am sure
his fear will bring him home and make him apply himself to me with all humility and kindness. For he is ever
underhand fain to use my interest and discretion to
make friends to compound these businesses, or to get an   35
order for the securing his person and honor.

SENTRY.

I believe verily, Mr. Courtall would have been so rude
to have killed him, if Mr. Freeman and the rest had
not civilly interposed their weapons.

LADY COCKWOOD.

Heavens forbid! Though he be a wicked man, I am   40
obliged in duty to love him. Whither did my cousins
go after we came home, Sentry?

SENTRY.

They are at the next door, madam, laughing and playing at lanterloo with my old Lady Love-youth and her
daughters.   45

LADY COCKWOOD.

I hope they will not come home then to interrupt my
affairs with Mr. Freeman.   *Knocking without.*
Hark! Somebody knocks. It may be him; run down
quickly.

35–36. *get . . . honor*] i.e., an order forbidding him to engage in a
duel.
    44. *lanterloo*] the older name of the card game later called loo.

SENTRY.

I fly, madam.   *Exit* Sentry.   50

LADY COCKWOOD.

Now if he has a real inclination for my person, I'll give
him a handsome opportunity to reveal it.

Enter Sentry *and* Freeman.

FREEMAN.

Your servant, madam.

LADY COCKWOOD.

Oh Mr. Freeman! This unlucky accident has robbed me
of all my quiet. I am almost distracted with thinking of   55
the danger Sir Oliver's dear life is in.

FREEMAN.

You need not fear, madam. All things will be reconciled
again tomorrow.

SENTRY.

You would not blame my lady's apprehensions, did you
but know the tenderness of her affections.   60

LADY COCKWOOD.

Mr. Courtall is a false and merciless man.

FREEMAN.

He has always owned a great respect for your ladyship,
and I never heard him mention you with the least dis-
honor.

LADY COCKWOOD.

He cannot without injuring the truth; Heaven knows my   65
innocence. I hope you did not let him know, sir, of
your coming hither.

FREEMAN.

I should never merit the happiness to wait upon you
again had I so abused this extraordinary favor, madam.

LADY COCKWOOD.

If I have done anything unbeseeming my honor, I hope   70
you will be just, sir, and impute it to my fear. I know
no man so proper to compose this unfortunate difference
as yourself, and if a lady's tears and prayers have power

to move you to compassion, I know you will employ your
utmost endeavor to preserve me my dear Sir Oliver.   75

FREEMAN.

Do not, madam, afflict yourself so much. I dare engage
my life, his life and honor shall be both secure.

LADY COCKWOOD.

You are truly noble, sir. I was so distracted with my
fears that I cannot well remember how we parted at the
Spring Garden.   80

FREEMAN.

We all divided, madam. After your ladyship and the
young ladies were gone together, Sir Oliver, Sir Joslin,
and the company with them took one boat, and Mr.
Courtall and I another.

LADY COCKWOOD.

Then I need not apprehend their meeting again tonight.   85

FREEMAN.

You need not, madam. I left Mr. Courtall in his chamber, wondering what should make Sir Oliver draw upon
him, and fretting and fuming about the trick that was
put upon us with the letters today.

LADY COCKWOOD.

Oh! I had almost forgot myself. I assure you, sir, those   90
letters were sent by one that has no inclination to be
an enemy of yours.   *Knocking below. Exit* Sentry.
Somebody knocks. If it be Sir Oliver, I am undone. He
will hate me mortally, if he does but suspect I use any
secret means to hinder him from justifying his reputa-   95
tion honorably to the world.

Enter Sentry.

SENTRY.

Oh madam! Here is Mr. Courtall below in the entry
discharging a coachman. I told him your ladyship was
busy, but he would not hear me, and I find, do what I
can, he will come up.   100

LADY COCKWOOD.

I would not willingly suspect you, sir.

FREEMAN.

> I have deceived him, madam, in my coming hither, and
> am as unwilling he should find me here as you can be.

LADY COCKWOOD.

> He will not believe my innocent business with you, but
> will raise a new scandal on my honor, and publish it to 105
> the whole town.

SENTRY.

> Let him step into the closet, madam.

LADY COCKWOOD.

> Quick, sir, quick. I beseech you. I will send him away
> again immediately.

Enter Courtall.

LADY COCKWOOD.

> Mr. Courtall! Have you no sense of honor nor modesty 110
> left? After so many injuries, to come into our house
> and without my approbation rudely press upon my re-
> tirement thus?

COURTALL.

> Pray, madam, hear my business.

LADY COCKWOOD.

> Thy business is maliciously to pursue my ruin. Thou 115
> comest with a base design to have Sir Oliver catch thee
> here, and destroy the only happiness I have.

COURTALL.

> I come, madam, to beg your pardon for the fault I did
> unwillingly commit, and to know of you the reason of
> Sir Oliver's quarrel to me.   120

LADY COCKWOOD.

> Thy guilty conscience is able to tell thee that, vain and
> ungrateful man!

COURTALL.

> I am innocent, madam, of all things that may offend
> him. And I am sure, if you would but hear me, I should
> remove the justice of your quarrel too.   125

LADY COCKWOOD.

> You are mistaken, sir, if you think I am concerned for

your going to the Spring Garden this evening. My quarrel is the same with Sir Oliver, and is so just that thou
deserv'st to be poisoned for what thou hast done.

COURTALL.

Pray, madam, let me know my fault.   130

LADY COCKWOOD.

I blush to think upon't. Sir Oliver, since we came from
the Bear, has heard something thou hast said concerning
me; but what it is, I could not get him to discover.
He told me 'twas enough for me to know he was satisfied of my innocence.   135

COURTALL.

This is mere passion, madam.

LADY COCKWOOD.

This is the usual revenge of such base men as thou art.
When they cannot compass their ends, with their ven-
omous tongues to blast the honor of a lady.

COURTALL.

This is a sudden alteration, madam. Within these few 140
hours you had a kinder opinion of me.

LADY COCKWOOD.

'Tis no wonder you brag of favors behind my back that
have the impudence to upbraid me with kindness to my
face. Dost thou think I could ever have a good thought
of thee, whom I have always found so treacherous in thy 145
friendship to Sir Oliver?

Knock at the door. Enter Sentry.

SENTRY.

Oh madam! Here is Sir Oliver come home.

LADY COCKWOOD.

Oh Heavens! I shall be believed guilty now, and he will
kill us both.

COURTALL.

I warrant you, madam, I'll defend your life.   150

He draws.

LADY COCKWOOD.

Oh! There will be murder, murder. For Heaven's sake,
sir, hide yourself in some corner or other.

COURTALL.

I'll step into that closet, madam.

SENTRY.

Hold, hold, sir; by no means. His pipes and his tobacco
box lie there, and he always goes in to fetch 'em.   155

LADY COCKWOOD.

Your malice will soon be at an end. Heaven knows what
will be the fatal consequence of your being found here.

SENTRY.

Madam, let him creep under the table. The carpet is
long enough to hide him.

LADY COCKWOOD.

Have you good nature enough to save the life and rep-   160
utation of a lady?

COURTALL.

Anything to oblige you, madam.

He goes under the table.

LADY COCKWOOD *(running to the closet).*

Be sure you do not stir, sir, whatsoever happens.

COURTALL.

Not unless he pulls me out by the ears.

SENTRY.

Good! He thinks my lady speaks to him.   165

Enter Sir Oliver.

LADY COCKWOOD.

My dear Sir Oliver.

SIR OLIVER.

I am unworthy of this kindness, madam.

LADY COCKWOOD.

Nay, I intend to chide you for your naughtiness anon.
But I cannot choose but hug thee and kiss thee a little
first. I was afraid I should never have thee alive within   170
these arms again.

SIR OLIVER.

Your goodness does so increase my shame, I know not
what to say, madam.

LADY COCKWOOD.

Well, I am glad I have thee safe at home. I will lock
thee up above in my chamber, and will not so much as 175
trust thee downstairs till there be an end to this quarrel.

SIR OLIVER.

I was so little myself, I knew not what I did; else I had
not exposed my person to so much danger before thy
face.

SENTRY.

'Twas cruelly done, sir, knowing the killing concerns my 180
lady has for you.

LADY COCKWOOD.

If Mr. Courtall had killed thee, I was resolved not to
survive thee. But before I had died, I would have dearly
revenged thy murder.

SIR OLIVER.

As soon as I had recollected myself a little, I could not 185
rest till I came home to give thee this satisfaction, that
I will do nothing without thy advice and approbation,
my dear. I know thy love makes thy life depend upon
mine, and it is unreasonable I should upon my own
rash head hazard that, though it be for the justification 190
of thy honor. Ud's me, I have let fall a China orange
that was recommended to me for one of the best that
came over this year. 'Slife, light the candle, Sentry. 'Tis
run under the table.   *Knock.*

LADY COCKWOOD.

Oh, I am not well!   200

*Sentry takes up the candle. There is a great knocking at the door.
She runs away with the candle.*

SENTRY.

Oh Heaven! Who's that that knocks so hastily?

SIR OLIVER.

Why, Sentry! Bring back the candle. Are you mad to

---

191. *China orange*] a sweet orange originally thought to have been
brought from China.

leave us in the dark, and your lady not well? How is it,
my dear?

LADY COCKWOOD.

For Heaven's sake, run after her, Sir Oliver; snatch the 200
candle out of her hand and teach her more manners.

SIR OLIVER.

I will, my dear.   ⌈Exit.

LADY COCKWOOD.

What shall I do? Was ever woman so unfortunate in the
management of affairs!

COURTALL.

What will become of me now?   205

LADY COCKWOOD.

It must be so. I had better trust my honor to the mercy
of them two than be betrayed to my husband. Mr.
Courtall, give me your hand quickly, I beseech you.

COURTALL.

Here, here, madam. What's to be done now?

LADY COCKWOOD.

I will put you into the closet, sir.   210

COURTALL.

He'll be coming in for his tobacco box and pipes.

LADY COCKWOOD.

Never fear that, sir.

FREEMAN *(out of the closet door)*.

Now shall I be discovered. Pox on your honorable intrigue. Would I were safe at Giffords.

LADY COCKWOOD.

Here, here, sir. This is the door. Whatsoever you feel, 215
be not frighted; for should you make the least disturb-
ance, you will destroy the life, and what is more the
honor of an unfortunate lady.

207. than] *Q3;* then *Q1–2.*

---

214. *Giffords*] Though Brett-Smith identifies this as an allusion to
a fashionable eating-house rather than to one of the era's famous
madams, the context seems to demand the latter reading.

COURTALL.

    So, so, if you have occasion to remove again, make no
ceremony, madam.   220

         Enter Sir Oliver, Sentry, Ariana, Gatty.

SIR OLIVER.

    Here is the candle. How dost thou, my dear?

LADY COCKWOOD.

    I could not imagine, Sentry, you had been so ill bred,
to run away and leave your master and me in the dark.

SENTRY.

    I thought there had been another candle upon the table,
madam.   225

LADY COCKWOOD.

    Good! You thought! You are always excusing of your
carelessness. Such another misdemeanor—

SIR OLIVER.

    Prithee my dear, forgive her.

LADY COCKWOOD.

    The truth is, I ought not to be very angry with her at
present. 'Tis a good-natured creature; she was so frighted, 230
for fear of thy being mischiefed in the Spring Garden,
that I verily believe she scarce knows what she does yet.

SIR OLIVER.

    Light the candle, Sentry, that I may look for my orange.

LADY COCKWOOD.

    You have been at my Lady Love-youth's, cousins, I hear.

ARIANA.

    She charged us to remember her service to you.   235

SIR OLIVER.

    So, here it is, my dear. I brought it home on purpose
for thee.

LADY COCKWOOD.

    'Tis a lovely orange indeed! Thank you, my dear. I am
so discomposed with the fright that I have had that I
would fain be at rest.   240

SIR OLIVER.

    Get a candle, Sentry. Will you go to bed, my dear?

LADY COCKWOOD.

    With all my heart, Sir Oliver. 'Tis late, cousins. You
    had best retire to your chamber too.

GATTY.

    We shall not stay long here, madam.

SIR OLIVER.

    Come, my dear.   245

LADY COCKWOOD.

    Good night, cousins.

GATTY. ARIANA.

    Your servant, madam.

                Exeunt Sir Oliver, Lady Cockwood, *and* Sentry.

ARIANA.

    I cannot but think of those letters, sister.

GATTY.

    That is, you cannot but think of Mr. Freeman, sister.
    I perceive he runs in thy head as much as a new gown 250
    used to do in the country, the night before 'tis expected
    from London.

ARIANA.

    You need not talk, for I am sure the losses of an unlucky
    gamester are not more his meditation, than Mr. Courtall
    is yours.   255

GATTY.

    It cannot last longer then the stain of a mulberry at
    most; the next season out that goes, and my heart cannot
    be long unfruitful, sure.

ARIANA.

    Well, I cannot believe they forged these letters. What
    should be their end?   260

GATTY.

    That you may easily guess at. But methinks they took
    a very improper way to compass it.

ARIANA.

    It looks more like the malice or jealousy of a woman,
    than the design of two witty men.

GATTY.

If this should prove a fetch of her ladyship's now, that 265
is playing the loving hypocrite above with her dear Sir
Oliver.

ARIANA.

How unluckily we were interrupted, when they were
going to show us the hand!

GATTY.

That might have discovered all. I have a small suspicion 270
that there has been a little familiarity between her ladyship and Mr. Courtall.

ARIANA.

Our finding of 'em together in the Exchange, and several passages I observed at the Bear, have almost made
me of the same opinion.   275

GATTY.

Yet I would fain believe the continuance of it is more
her desire than his inclination. That which makes me
mistrust him most is her knowing we made 'em an
appointment.

ARIANA.

If she were jealous of Mr. Courtall, she would not be 280
jealous of Mr. Freeman too; they both pretend to have
received letters.

GATTY.

There is something in it more than we are able to
imagine. Time will make it out, I hope, to the advantage
of the gentlemen.   285

ARIANA.

I would gladly have it so. For I believe, should they give
us a just cause, we should find it a hard task to hate
them.

GATTY.

How I love the song I learnt t'other day, since I saw
them in the Mulberry Garden!   *She sings.* 290
    To little or no purpose I spent many days,
    In ranging the Park, th'Exchange, and th'plays;
    For ne'er in my rambles till now did I prove

So lucky to meet with the man I could love.
Oh! how I am pleased when I think on this man,   295
That I find I must love, let me do what I can!
How long I shall love him, I can no more tell
Than had I a fever, when I should be well.
My passion shall kill me before I will show it,
And yet I would give all the world he did know it;   300
But oh how I sigh, when I think, should he woo me,
I cannot deny what I know would undo me!

ARIANA.

Fie, sister, thou art so wanton.

GATTY.

I hate to dissemble when I need not. 'Twould look as
affected in us to be reserved now we're alone as for a 305
player to maintain the character she acts in the tiring
room.

ARIANA.

Prithee sing a good song.

GATTY.

Now art thou for a melancholy madrigal, composed
by some amorous coxcomb, who swears in all companies 310
he loves his mistress so well that he would not do her
injury, were she willing to grant him the favor, and
it may be is sot enough to believe he would oblige her
in keeping his oath, too.

ARIANA.

Well, I will reach thee thy guitar out of the closet, 315
to take thee off of this subject.

GATTY.

I'd rather be a nun than a lover at thy rate; devotion
is not able to make me half so serious as love has made
thee already.

Ariana *opens the closet,* Courtall *and* Freeman *come out.*

COURTALL.

Ha, Freeman! Is this your business with a lawyer? Here's 320
a new discovery, i'faith!   *They shriek and run out.*

298. Than] *Q3;* Then *Q1–2.*

FREEMAN.

Peace, man. I will satisfy your jealousy hereafter; since
we have made this lucky discovery, let us mind the present business.

Courtall *and* Freeman *catch the ladies, and bring them back.*

Nay, ladies, now we have caught you, there is no escap- 325
ing till we're come to a right understanding.

Enter Lady Cockwood *and* Sir Oliver *and* Sentry.

FREEMAN.

Come, never blush, we are as loving as you can be for
your hearts, I assure you.

COURTALL.

Had it not been our good fortunes to have been con-
cealed here, you would have had ill nature enough to 330
dissemble with us at least a fortnight longer.

LADY COCKWOOD.

What's the matter with you here? Are you mad, cousins?
Bless me, Mr. Courtall and Mr. Freeman in our house
at these unseasonable hours!

SIR OLIVER.

Fetch me down my long sword, Sentry; I lay my life 335
Courtall has been tempting the honor of the young
ladies.

LADY COCKWOOD.

Oh my dear!   *She holds him.*

GATTY.

We are almost scared out of our wits; my sister went
to reach my guitar out of the closet, and found 'em 340
both shut up there.

LADY COCKWOOD.

Come, come. This will not serve your turn. I am afraid
you had a design secretly to convey 'em into your
chamber. Well, I will have no more of these doings in
my family, my dear. Sir Joslin shall remove these girls 345
tomorrow.

FREEMAN.

You injure the young ladies, madam. Their surprise
shows their innocence.

COURTALL.

If anybody be to blame, it is Mrs. Sentry.

SENTRY.

What mean you, sir? Heaven knows I know no more 350
of their being here—

COURTALL.

Nay, nay, Mrs. Sentry. You need not be ashamed to
own the doing of a couple of young gentlemen such a
good office.

SENTRY.

Do not think to put your tricks upon me, sir. 355

COURTALL.

Understanding by Mrs. Sentry, madam, that these young
ladies would very likely sit and talk in the dining room
an hour before they went to bed, of the accidents of the
day, and being impatient to know whether that unlucky
business which happened in the Spring Garden, about 360
the letters, had quite destroyed our hopes of gaining
their esteem, for a small sum of money Mr. Freeman
and I obtained the favor of her to shut us up where
we might overhear 'em.

LADY COCKWOOD.

Is this the truth, Sentry? 365

SENTRY.

I humbly beg your pardon, madam.

LADY COCKWOOD.

A lady's honor is not safe that keeps a servant so subject
to corruption; I will turn her out of my service for this.

SIR OLIVER [aside].

Good! I was suspicious their businesses had been with
my lady, at first. 370

LADY COCKWOOD [aside].

Now will I be in charity with him again for putting
this off so handsomely.

–111–

SIR OLIVER.

Hark you, my dear, shall I forbid Mr. Courtall my house?

LADY COCKWOOD.

Oh! By no means, my dear. I had forgot to tell thee, since I acquainted thee with that business, I have been 375 discoursing with my Lady Love-youth, and she blamed me infinitely for letting thee know it, and laughed exceedingly at me, believing Mr. Courtall intended thee no injury, and told me 'twas only a harmless gallantry, which his French breeding has used him to.   380

SIR OLIVER.

Faith, I am apt enough to believe it. For on my conscience, he is a very honest fellow. Ned Courtall! How the devil came it about that thee and I fell to sa, sa, in the Spring Garden?

COURTALL.

You are best able to resolve yourself that, Sir Oliver. 385

SIR OLIVER.

Well, the devil take me if I had the least unkindness for thee. Prithee let us embrace and kiss, and be as good friends as ever we were, dear rogue.

COURTALL.

I am so reasonable, Sir Oliver, that I will ask no other satisfaction for the injury you have done me.   390

FREEMAN.

Here's the letter, madam.

ARIANA.

Sister, look here, do you know this hand?

GATTY.

'Tis Sentry's.

LADY COCKWOOD [aside].

Oh Heavens! I shall be ruined yet.

GATTY.

She has been the contriver of all this mischief.   395

COURTALL.

Nay, now you lay too much to her charge in this. She was but my lady's secretary, I assure you; she has discovered the whole plot to us.

SENTRY [*aside*].

What does he mean?

LADY COCKWOOD [*aside*].

Will he betray me at last?   400

COURTALL.

My lady, being in her nature severely virtuous, is, it
seems, offended at the innocent freedom you take in
rambling up and down by yourselves; which made
her, out of a tenderness to your reputations, counterfeit
these letters, in hopes to fright you to that reservedness 405
which she approves of.

LADY COCKWOOD [*aside*].

This has almost redeemed my opinion of his honor.
—Cousins, the little regard you had to the good counsel
I gave you, puts me upon this business.

GATTY.

Pray, madam, what was it Mrs. Gazette told you con- 410
cerning us?

LADY COCKWOOD.

Nothing, nothing, cousins. What I told you of Mr. Courtall was mere invention, the better to carry on my
design for your good.

COURTALL.

Freeman! Pray what brought you hither?   415

FREEMAN.

A kind summons from her ladyship.

COURTALL.

Why did you conceal it from me?

FREEMAN.

I was afraid thy peevish jealousy might have destroyed
the design I had of getting an opportunity to clear
ourselves to the young ladies.   420

COURTALL.

Fortune has been our friend in that beyond expectation.
(*To the ladies.*) I hope, ladies, you are satisfied of our
innocence now.

GATTY.

Well, had you been found guilty of the letters, we were

-113-

resolved to have counterfeited two contracts under your 425
hands, and have suborned witnesses to swear to 'em.

ARIANA.

That had been a full revenge; for I know you would
think it as great a scandal to be thought to have an
inclination for marriage as we should to be believed
willing to take our freedom without it. 430

COURTALL.

The more probable thing, ladies, had been only to
pretend a promise; we have now and then courage
enough to venture so far for a valuable consideration.

GATTY.

The truth is, such experienced gentlemen as you are
seldom mortgage your persons without it be to redeem 435
your estates.

COURTALL.

'Tis a mercy we have 'scaped the mischief so long, and
are like to do penance only for our own sins; most families are a wedding behind hand in the world, which
makes so many young men fooled into wives to pay 440
their father's debts. All the happiness a gentleman can
desire is to live at liberty, till he be forced that way to
pay his own.

FREEMAN.

Ladies, you know we are not ignorant of the good intentions you have toward us; pray let us treat a little. 445

GATTY.

I hope you are not in so desperate a condition as to
have a good opinion of marriage, are you?

ARIANA.

'Tis to as little purpose to treat with us of anything
under that, as it for those kind ladies, that have obliged
you with a valuable consideration, to challenge the 450
performance of your promise.

SIR OLIVER.

Well, and how, and how, my dear Ned, goes the busi-

---

439. *wedding . . . world*] a reference to the fact that weddings, in
this period, were frequently financial rather than romantic unions.

ness between you and these ladies? Are you like to drive
a bargain?

COURTALL.

Faith, Sir Oliver, we are about it.   455

SIR OLIVER.

And cannot agree, I warrant you; they are for having
you take a lease for life, and you are for being tenants
at will, Ned, is it not so?

GATTY.

These gentlemen have found it so convenient lying
in lodgings, they'll hardly venture on the trouble of 460
taking a house of their own.

COURTALL.

A pretty country seat, madam, with a handsome parcel
of land, and other necessaries belonging to't, may tempt
us; but for a town tenement that has but one poor conveniency, we are resolved we'll never deal.   465

                              A noise of music without.

SIR OLIVER.

Hark! My Brother Jolly's come home.

ARIANA.

Now, gentlemen, you had best look to yourselves, and
come to an agreement with us quickly; for I'll lay
my life, my uncle has brought home a couple of fresh
chapmen that will outbid you.   470

              Enter Sir Joslin *with music.*

SIR JOSLIN.

Hey boys!   *Dance.*

                    Sings.

          A catch and a glass,
          A fiddle and a lass,
          What more would an honest man have?
          Hang your temperate sot,   475
          Who would seem what he's not;
          'Tis I am wise, he's but grave.

---

470. *chapmen*] traders.

SIR JOSLIN.

What's here? Mr. Courtall and Mr. Freeman!

SIR OLIVER.

Oh man! Here has been the prettiest, the luckiest
discovery on all sides! We are all good friends again.　480

SIR JOSLIN.

Hark you Brother Cockwood, I have got Madam Rampant; Rake-hell and she are without.

SIR OLIVER.

Oh Heavens! Dear Brother Jolly, send her away immediately. My lady has such an aversion to a naughty woman
that she will swound if she does but see her.　485

SIR JOSLIN.

Faith, I was hard put to't. I wanted a lover, and rather
than I would break my old wont, I dressed up Rampant
in a suit I bought of Rake-hell; but since this good
company's here I'll send her away.

Enter Rake-hell [*and* Rampant].

My little Rake-hell, come hither; you see here are two　490
powerful rivals; therefore for fear of kicking, or a
worse disaster, take Rampant with you, and be going
quickly.

RAKE-HELL.

Your humble servant, sir.　　　*Exit* Rake-hell *and* Rampant.

COURTALL.

You may hereafter spare yourself this labor, Sir Joslin;　495
Mr. Freeman and I have vowed ourselves humble servants to these ladies.

FREEMAN.

I hope we shall have your approbation, sir.

SIR JOSLIN.

Nay, if you have a mind to commit matrimony, I'll send
for a canonical sir shall dispatch you presently.　500

FREEMAN.

You cannot do better.

487. than] *Q3;* then *Q1–2.*　　489.1.] *Q3; in Q1–2 follows* bought
　　　　　　　　　　　　　　　(l. 488).

COURTALL.

What think you of taking us in the humor? Consideration may be your foe, ladies.

ARIANA.

Come, gentlemen, I'll make you a fair proposition; since you have made a discovery of our inclinations, my 505 sister and I will be content to admit you in the quality of servants.

GATTY.

And if after a month's experience of your good behavior, upon serious thoughts, you have courage enough to engage further, we will accept of the challenge, and 510 believe you men of honor.

SIR JOSLIN.

Well spoke i'faith, girls; and is it a match, boys?

COURTALL.

If the heart of man be not very deceitful, 'tis very likely it may be so.

FREEMAN.

A month is a tedious time, and will be a dangerous 515 trial of our resolutions; but I hope we shall not repent before marriage, whate'er we do after.

SIR JOSLIN.

How stand matters between you and your lady, Brother Cockwood? Is there peace on all sides?

SIR OLIVER.

Perfect concord, man. I will tell thee all that has hap- 520 pened since I parted from thee, when we are alone; 'twill make thee laugh heartily. Never man was so happy in a virtuous and loving lady!

SIR JOSLIN.

Though I have led Sir Oliver astray this day or two, I hope you will not exclude me the Act of Oblivion, 525 madam.

LADY COCKWOOD.

The nigh relation I have to you, and the respect I know Sir Oliver has for you, makes me forget all that

has passed, sir; but pray be not the occasion of any
new transgressions.   530

SENTRY.

I hope, Mr. Courtall, since my endeavors to serve you
have ruined me in the opinion of my lady, you will
intercede for a reconciliation.

COURTALL.

Most willingly, Mrs. Sentry. —Faith, madam, since
things have fallen out so luckily, you must needs receive 535
your woman into favor again.

LADY COCKWOOD.

Her crime is unpardonable, sir.

SENTRY.

Upon solemn protestations, madam, that the gentlemen's
intentions were honorable, and having reason to believe
the young ladies had no aversion to their inclinations, 540
I was of the opinion I should have been ill natured
if I had not assisted 'em in the removing those difficul-
ties that delayed their happiness.

SIR OLIVER.

Come, come, girl, confess how many guineas prevailed
upon your easy nature.   545

SENTRY.

Ten, an't please you, sir.

SIR OLIVER.

'Slife, a sum able to corrupt an honest man in office!
Faith you must forgive her, my dear.

LADY COCKWOOD.

If it be your pleasure, Sir Oliver, I cannot but be obedient.

SENTRY.

If Sir Oliver, madam, should ask me to see this gold, 550
all may be discovered yet.

LADY COCKWOOD.

If he does, I will give thee ten guineas out of my
cabinet.

SENTRY [aside].

I shall take care to put him upon't; 'tis fit that I, who

have bore all the blame, should have some reasonable 555
reward for't.

COURTALL.

I hope, madam, you will not envy me the happiness
I am to enjoy with your fair relation.

LADY COCKWOOD.

Your ingenuity and goodness, sir, have made a perfect
atonement for you.   560

COURTALL.

Pray, madam, what was your business with Mr. Freeman?

LADY COCKWOOD.

Only to oblige him to endeavor a reconciliation between
you and Sir Oliver. For though I was resolved never
to see your face again, it was death to me to think your
life was in danger.   565

SENTRY.

What a miraculous come-off is this, madam!

LADY COCKWOOD.

It has made me so truly sensible of those dangers to
which an aspiring lady must daily expose her honor, that
I am resolved to give over the great business of this
town, and hereafter modestly confine myself to the   570
humble affairs of my own family.

COURTALL.

'Tis a very pious resolution, madam, and the better to
confirm you in it, pray entertain an able chaplain.

LADY COCKWOOD.

Certainly fortune was never before so unkind to the ambition of a lady.   575

SIR JOSLIN.

Come, boys, faith we will have a dance before we go
to bed. Sly-girl and Mad-cap, give me your hands, that
I may give 'em to the gentlemen. A parson shall join
you ere long, and then you will have authority to dance
to some purpose. Brother Cockwood, take out your   580
lady, I am for Mrs. Sentry.

We'll foot it and side it, my pretty little Miss,

582. side it] *Q1 corr., Q2–3;* side *Q1 uncorr.*

And when we are aweary, we'll lie down and kiss.
Play away, boys.

They dance.

COURTALL *(to* Gatty*).*

Now shall I sleep as little without you, as I should do 585
with you. Madam, expectation makes me almost as restless as jealousy.

FREEMAN.

Faith, let us dispatch this business; yet I never could
find the pleasure of waiting for a dish of meat when a
man was heartily hungry.   590

GATTY.

Marrying in this heat would look as ill as fighting in
your drink.

ARIANA.

And be no more a proof of love, then t'other is of
valor.

SIR JOSLIN.

Never trouble your heads further; since I perceive you 595
are all agreed on the matter, let me alone to hasten the
ceremony. Come, gentlemen, lead 'em to their chambers;
Brother Cockwood, do you show the way with your lady.
Ha Mrs. Sentry!   *Sings.*

   I gave my love a green gown   600
   I'th' merry month of May,
   And down she fell as wantonly
   As a tumbler does at play.

Hey boys, lead away boys.

SIR OLIVER.

Give me thy hand, my virtuous, my dear.   605
  Henceforwards may our mutual loves increase,
  And when we are a-bed, we'll sign the peace.

        Exeunt omnes.

---

583. aweary] *Q1;* a weary *Q2;* 590. hungry] *Q1 corr., Q2–3;* a
weary *Q3.*   hungry *Q1 uncorr.*

Appendix

Chronology

Approximate years are indicated by *. Dates for plays are those on which they were first made public, either on stage or in print.

Political and Literary Events	*Life and Major Works of Etherege*
1631	
Death of Donne.	
John Dryden born.	
1633	
Samuel Pepys born.	
1635	
	George Etherege born.*
1640	
Aphra Behn born.*	
1641	
William Wycherley born.*	
1642	
First Civil War began (ended 1646).	
Theaters closed by Parliament.	
Thomas Shadwell born.*	
1648	
Second Civil War.	
Nathaniel Lee born.*	
1649	
Execution of Charles I.	
1650	
Jeremy Collier born.	
1651	
Hobbes' *Leviathan* published.	
1652	
First Dutch War began (ended 1654).	

Thomas Otway born.

1656

D'Avenant's *THE SIEGE OF RHODES* performed at Rutland House.

1657

John Dennis born.

1658

Death of Oliver Cromwell.

D'Avenant's *THE CRUELTY OF THE SPANIARDS IN PERU* performed at the Cockpit.

1660

Restoration of Charles II.

Theatrical patents granted to Thomas Killigrew and Sir William D'Avenant, authorizing them to form, respectively, the King's and the Duke of York's Companies.

Pepys began his diary.

1661

Cowley's *THE CUTTER OF COLEMAN STREET*.

D'Avenant's *THE SIEGE OF RHODES* (expanded to two parts).

1662

Charter granted to the Royal Society.

1663

Dryden's *THE WILD GALLANT*.

Tuke's *THE ADVENTURES OF FIVE HOURS*.

1664

Sir John Vanbrugh born. *THE COMICAL REVENGE.*

Dryden's *THE RIVAL LADIES*.

Dryden and Howard's *THE INDIAN QUEEN*.

1665

Second Dutch War began (ended 1667).

Great Plague.
Dryden's *THE INDIAN EM-
PEROR.*
Orrery's *MUSTAPHA.*

1666
Fire of London.
Death of James Shirley.

1667
Jonathan Swift born.
Milton's *Paradise Lost* published.
Sprat's *The History of the Royal
Society* published.
Dryden's *SECRET LOVE.*

1668
Death of D'Avenant.
Dryden made Poet Laureate.
Dryden's *An Essay of Dramatic
Poesy* published.
Shadwell's *THE SULLEN
LOVERS.*

SHE WOULD IF SHE COULD.
Travels to Constantinople as secretary to the English ambassador
to Turkey.

1669
Pepys terminated his diary.
Susanna Centlivre born.

1670
William Congreve born.
Dryden's *THE CONQUEST OF
GRANADA,* Part I.

1671
Dorset Garden Theatre (Duke's
Company) opened.
Colley Cibber born.
Milton's *Paradise Regained* and
Samson Agonistes published.
Dryden's *THE CONQUEST OF
GRANADA,* Part II.
THE REHEARSAL, by the Duke
of Buckingham and others.
Wycherley's *LOVE IN A WOOD.*

Returns to London.

1672
Third Dutch War began (ended
1674).

Joseph Addison born.
Richard Steele born.
Dryden's *MARRIAGE A LA MODE.*

1674
New Drury Lane Theatre (King's Company) opened.
Death of Milton.
Nicholas Rowe born.
Thomas Rymer's *Reflections on Aristotle's Treatise of Poesy* (translation of Rapin) published.

1675
Dryden's *AURENG-ZEBE.*
Wycherley's *THE COUNTRY WIFE.**

1676
Otway's *DON CARLOS.*   *THE MAN OF MODE.*
Shadwell's *THE VIRTUOSO.*
Wycherley's *THE PLAIN DEALER.*

1677
Rymer's *Tragedies of the Last Age Considered* published.
Aphra Behn's *THE ROVER.*
Dryden's *ALL FOR LOVE.*
Lee's *THE RIVAL QUEENS.*

1678
Popish Plot.
George Farquhar born.
Bunyan's *Pilgrim's Progress* (Part I) published.

1679
Exclusion Bill introduced.   Is knighted and marries a "rich
Death of Thomas Hobbes.   old widow."*
Death of Roger Boyle, Earl of Orrery.
Charles Johnson born.

1680
Death of Samuel Butler.

Death of John Wilmot, Earl of
Rochester.
Dryden's *THE SPANISH FRIAR.*
Lee's *LUCIUS JUNIUS BRUTUS.*
Otway's *THE ORPHAN.*

1681
Charles II dissolved Parliament at
Oxford.
Dryden's *Absalom and Achitophel*
published.
Tate's adaptation of *KING LEAR.*

1682
The King's and the Duke of
York's Companies merged into
the United Company.
Dryden's *The Medal, MacFleck-*
noe, and *Religio Laici* published.
Otway's *VENICE PRESERVED.*

Receives a pension from the Duke
of York, later James II.

1683
Rye House Plot.
Death of Thomas Killigrew.
Crowne's *CITY POLITIQUES.*

1685
Death of Charles II; accession of
James II.
Revocation of the Edict of Nantes.
The Duke of Monmouth's Re-
bellion.
Death of Otway.
John Gay born.
Crowne's *SIR COURTLY NICE.*
Dryden's *ALBION AND AL-*
BANIUS.

Appointed envoy to Ratisbon by
James II; arrives at Ratisbon in
November.

1687
Death of the Duke of Bucking-
ham.
Dryden's *The Hind and the Pan-*
ther published.
Newton's *Principia* published.

1688
The Revolution.

Alexander Pope born.
Shadwell's *THE SQUIRE OF ALSATIA*.

1689
The War of the League of Augsburg began (ended 1697).
Toleration Act.
Death of Aphra Behn.
Shadwell made Poet Laureate.
Dryden's *DON SEBASTIAN*.
Shadwell's *BURY FAIR*.

Leaves Ratisbon after the accession of William III; goes to Paris.

1690
Battle of the Boyne.
Locke's *Two Treatises of Government* and *An Essay Concerning Human Understanding* published.

1691
Langbaine's *An Account of the English Dramatic Poets* published.

Dies in Paris.*

1692
Death of Lee.
Death of Shadwell.
Tate made Poet Laureate.

1693
George Lillo born.*
Rymer's *A Short View of Tragedy* published.
Congreve's *THE OLD BACHELOR*.

1694
Death of Queen Mary.
Southerne's *THE FATAL MARRIAGE*.

1695
Group of actors led by Thomas Betterton left Drury Lane and established a new company at Lincoln's Inn Fields.
Congreve's *LOVE FOR LOVE*.
Southerne's *OROONOKO*.

1696

Cibber's *LOVE'S LAST SHIFT*.

Vanbrugh's *THE RELAPSE*.

1697

Treaty of Ryswick ended the War of the League of Augsburg.

Charles Macklin born.

Congreve's *THE MOURNING BRIDE*.

Vanbrugh's *THE PROVOKED WIFE*.

1698

Collier controversy started with the publication of *A Short View of the Immorality and Profaneness of the English Stage*.

1699

Farquhar's *THE CONSTANT COUPLE*.

1700

Death of Dryden.

Blackmore's *Satire against Wit* published.

Congreve's *THE WAY OF THE WORLD*.

1701

Act of Settlement.

War of the Spanish Succession began (ended 1713).

Death of James II.

Rowe's *TAMERLANE*.

Steele's *THE FUNERAL*.

1702

Death of William III; accession of Anne.

The Daily Courant began publication.

Cibber's *SHE WOULD AND SHE WOULD NOT*.

1703

Death of Samuel Pepys.

Rowe's *THE FAIR PENITENT*.

1704

Capture of Gibraltar; Battle of Blenheim.

Defoe's *The Review* began publication (1704–1713).

Swift's *A Tale of a Tub* and *The Battle of the Books* published.

Cibber's *THE CARELESS HUSBAND*.

1705

Haymarket Theatre opened.

Steele's *THE TENDER HUSBAND*.

1706

Battle of Ramillies.

Farquhar's *THE RECRUITING OFFICER*.

1707

Union of Scotland and England.

Death of Farquhar.

Henry Fielding born.

Farquhar's *THE BEAUX' STRATAGEM*.

1708

Downes' *Roscius Anglicanus* published.

1709

Samuel Johnson born.

Rowe's edition of Shakespeare published.

The Tatler began publication (1709–1711).

Centlivre's *THE BUSY BODY*.

1711

Shaftesbury's *Characteristics* published.

The Spectator began publication (1711–1712).

Pope's *An Essay on Criticism* published.

1713

Treaty of Utrecht ended the War
of the Spanish Succession.
Addison's *CATO*.

1714

Death of Anne; accession of
George I.
Steele became Governor of Drury
Lane.
John Rich assumed management
of Lincoln's Inn Fields.
Centlivre's *THE WONDER: A
WOMAN KEEPS A SECRET*.
Rowe's *JANE SHORE*.

1715

Jacobite Rebellion.
Death of Tate.
Rowe made Poet Laureate.
Death of Wycherley.

1716

Addison's *THE DRUMMER*.

1717

David Garrick born.
Cibber's *THE NON-JUROR*.
Gay, Pope, and Arbuthnot's
*THREE HOURS AFTER MAR-
RIAGE*.

1718

Death of Rowe.
Centlivre's *A BOLD STROKE
FOR A WIFE*.

1719

Death of Addison.
Defoe's *Robinson Crusoe* pub-
lished.
Young's *BUSIRIS, KING OF
EGYPT*.

1720

South Sea Bubble.
Samuel Foote born.
Steele suspended from the Gov-

ernorship of Drury Lane (restored 1721).

Little Theatre in the Haymarket opened.

Steele's *The Theatre* (periodical) published.

Hughes' *THE SIEGE OF DA-MASCUS*.

1721

Walpole became first Minister.

1722

Steele's *THE CONSCIOUS LOVERS*.

1723

Death of Susanna Centlivre.

Death of D'Urfey.

1725

Pope's edition of Shakespeare published.

1726

Death of Jeremy Collier.

Death of Vanbrugh.

Law's *Unlawfulness of Stage Entertainments* published.

Swift's *Gulliver's Travels* published.

1727

Death of George I; accession of George II.

Death of Sir Isaac Newton.

Arthur Murphy born.

1728

Pope's *The Dunciad* (first version) published.

Cibber's *THE PROVOKED HUSBAND* (expansion of Vanbrugh's fragment *A JOURNEY TO LONDON*).

Gay's *THE BEGGAR'S OPERA*.

1729

Goodman's Fields Theatre opened.

Death of Congreve.
Death of Steele.
Edmund Burke born.
1730.
Cibber made Poet Laureate.
Oliver Goldsmith born.
Thomson's *The Seasons* published.
Fielding's *THE AUTHOR'S FARCE*.
Fielding's *TOM THUMB* (revised as *THE TRAGEDY OF TRAGEDIES*, 1731).
1731
Death of Defoe.
Fielding's *THE GRUB-STREET OPERA*.
Lillo's *THE LONDON MERCHANT*.
1732
Covent Garden Theatre opened.
Death of Gay.
George Colman the elder born.
Fielding's *THE COVENT GARDEN TRAGEDY*.
Fielding's *THE MODERN HUSBAND*.
Charles Johnson's *CAELIA*.
1733
Pope's *An Essay on Man* (Epistles I–III) published (Epistle IV, 1734).
1734
Death of Dennis.
The Prompter began publication (1734–1736).
Theobald's edition of Shakespeare published.
Fielding's *DON QUIXOTE IN ENGLAND*.
1736
Fielding led the "Great Mogul's Company of Comedians" at the Little Theatre in the Haymarket

(1736–1737).
Fielding's *PASQUIN.*
Lillo's *FATAL CURIOSITY.*

1737
The Stage Licensing Act.
Dodsley's *THE KING AND THE MILLER OF MANSFIELD.*
Fielding's *THE HISTORICAL REGISTER FOR 1736.*

Scarlatti
K. 430, 445
Basis of Thomasini
"Good Natured Ladies"
or "Good Humor'd Ladies"